Andrew Stevenson was born in Canada and brought up in Hong Kong, India, Kenya, Scotland, Singapore and Malaysia before attending university in Canada and France. He has worked in Canada, Tanzania and Norway as banker, economist for the United Nations, African safari operator and owner of a Norwegian adventure company. When he isn't travelling he writes in Bermuda.

Andrew is also the author of *Annapurna Circuit: Himalayan Journey.*

KIWI TRACKS

A NEW ZEALAND JOURNEY

ANDREW STEVENSON

LONELY PLANET PUBLICATIONS
Melbourne • Oakland • London • Paris

Kiwi Tracks: A New Zealand Journey

Published by Lonely Planet Publications
Head Office: PO Box 617, Hawthorn, Vic 3122, Australia
Branches: 150 Linden Street, Oakland, CA 94607, USA
10a Spring Place, London NW5 3BH, UK
1 rue Dahomey, 75011, Paris, France

Published 1999

Printed by The Bookmaker Pty Ltd
Printed in China

Map by Tony Fankhauser
Designed by Tamsin Wilson
Edited by Lucy Sussex

National Library of Australia Cataloguing in Publication Data

Stevenson, Andrew.
Kiwi tracks: a New Zealand journey.

ISBN 0 86442 787 5.

1. Stevenson, Andrew – Journeys – New Zealand.
2. New Zealand – Description and travel. I. Title.

919.9304

Text © Andrew Stevenson 1999
Map © Lonely Planet 1999

Dedicated to the memory of my brother, Kevin.

CONTENTS

NORTH ISLAND

January

February

ACKNOWLEDGEMENTS

My appreciation to all the Kiwis who made tramping around New Zealand for four months the wonderful experience that it was. I'm definitely coming back.

Thanks are due to several friends who were coerced into reading successive drafts and who sometimes made rude but inevitably helpful comments: Kirsten Badenduck, Valerie Beatts, Sacha Blackburne, Than Butterfield, Wenche Fosslien, Sue Holland, Kerry Mahony, Sue Mills, Elisabeth Montgomery, Jennifer Schelter, Tania Stafford and Ingrid Zondervan. Thanks to Lucy Sussex for the final cross-examination. Any remaining errors are of course mine. Thanks to the staff at the Kathmandu Guest House for the familial atmosphere that made writing there so much easier, and to Valerie Beatts for lending me Per Ketet.

Thanks to Susan Keogh at Lonely Planet for accepting a dusty disc from a lowly backpacker making his way around Australia.

Finally, thanks to Mum for instilling in us the confidence that we could do whatever we wanted, and for picking up the pieces when we couldn't.

SOUTH ISLAND

NOVEMBER

※

FIORDLAND

I explore Te Anau, still jet lagged by the 25-hour flight from London to Christchurch, and a full day's hitchhiking. Snow-covered jagged mountains and a wind-swept, glacier-gauged lake front the sleepy municipal centre of Fiordland. The scenery and people look strangely familiar, as if I hadn't flown to the other side of the world at all. I could be back in the American Rockies or in Norway.

Hungry and cold, I find a pub. I settle on a barstool, lean over the counter and reflect on the day. There are few places in the world where you can still hitchhike safely, if at all. It was rumoured to be ridiculously easy in New Zealand and it was. The cars, some of them classic British models from the fifties and sixties, almost formed a line to pick me up, as if the hospitable Kiwis were competing to chauffeur me around. One driver not only went out of her way to drop me off at the backpackers, but she had thrown in a meal as well.

I'm psyched to be here, with the conspicuous wide-eyes of a traveller newly arrived somewhere far from home. The barmaid, on the other hand, studies me with the glazed look of a professional.

'Anyone sitting here?' I ask, with the cultivated nonchalance of a veteran globetrotter.

The bar is empty.

'Yeah, go for it,' she replies, poker-faced. 'What'll you have, mate?'

'Your special,' I reply casually, trying not to sound too much a foreigner.

'What special?'

'You know, your special.'

'Which special?' she reiterates impatiently. I detect a hint of disdain.

I blink, taken aback. She has called my bluff already. Nervous, I squirm to the edge of the barstool. Outside is a blackboard advertising their daily special. I look out the window. Unfortunately, it is facing the wrong way.

'You've a blackboard out there with "Daily Special" written on it. I'll have your daily special,' I repeat with a faked casual smile, nodding enthusiastically to encourage her. After the consistent friendliness and hospitality I have experienced since arriving in New Zealand, I am surprised by her apparent hostility.

'What's it say exactly?' she asks.

I am on shaky ground. I cannot remember exactly what the sign says. 'Some kind of special. I don't really know,' I admit timidly. She's sussed me out: I am not a cool dude who just breezed in for a beer.

'Well, I don't know what you want either,' she says, rolling her eyes, hands on her hips like a teacher mocking the class dunce.

I have had a great day, and this arm-wrestler of a stroppy barmaid is wrecking it. Where did they find her? I count to ten and look at her eye to eye, *mano a mano*. There is no mistaking her antagonism. If looks could kill, I would be dead and buried six feet under.

'Do you work here?' I ask, tempting fate.

'Ah come on, don't give me that.' She grabs a menu. 'Here, take a look at what you want.' She tosses the menu on the counter and jabs her finger at it so hard I am surprised her finger doesn't snap in two. I duck, thinking she may throw a punch.

'It's a toasted something or other. With a beer. The special,' I repeat.

'I still don't know what you want!'

I lean back out of range just in case she changes her mind about the punch. She's either having a bad day or there is some kind of basic cross-cultural communication problem here, despite the superficial similarity of language. Maybe she is from another planet, although that is usually what I am accused of. 'Look, it's not worth it. I'll go somewhere else.'

'Ah come on mate, don't go over the top. We're not playing for bloody sheep stations, you know.'

To retain some semblance of dignity as I retreat out the door, I assume what I hope is a plausible imitation of a John Wayne tough-guy strolling out of a cowboy saloon, although I'm half Wayne's size and a lot skinnier. I glance nervously at the black-board to see what I am missing out on with the special.

'Daily Special. Toasted Sammie and a Beer.'

What the hell is a 'sammie'? Local fish? I thought samis were reindeer herders in the north of Scandinavia. I wander aimlessly on the scenic path skirting the lake, the view not seeming quite as idyllic as it did a few minutes ago. Exhausted from the confrontation, I withdraw to the backpackers and flop on my bed. I recount the episode to my Australian roommate. He wears a T-shirt with the slogan, 'I support two teams: The Aussies and whoever is playing against the Kiwis'.

He explains: 'A "sammie" is a sandwich.' He puts down the cricket magazine he has been reading while cutting his toenails with the scissors on his penknife. 'Bloody Kiwi chicks,' he adds, replacing the scissors, and opening the knife blade to remove dirt from under his fingernails. 'Legs thicker than tree trunks. Good genetic stock for rugby players and handy wives to have around the farm, but don't expect to fall in love with one.'

The barmaid was only asking me what kind of toasted sandwich I wanted. Turkey, tuna, ham, chicken, beef or cheese? She probably talks like that to all her regular Kiwi customers. If I was a typical cool All Blacks Kiwi rugby player whose father owned a million-acre sheep station, I would have thought, 'What a friendly barmaid,' and enjoyed the banter. Next time I will slam a fist on the counter. No, I'll slam two tiny fists on the counter and tell her in no uncertain terms what kind of goddamned sammie I want.

If I dare go back there again.

MILFORD TRACK

Every bit of Kiwi tourist literature refers to the Milford Track as being 'the finest walk in the world'. This much-repeated phrase first appeared in an article by poet Blanche Baughan, published by the London *Spectator* in 1908. The Milford Track runs through Fiordland National Park, from the head of Lake Te Anau to Milford Sound. Fiordland National Park is part of the Southwest New Zealand World Heritage Area, which includes fiords, glacier-cut gorges, lakes and hanging valleys. It also provides, according to all the tourist literature, some of the best examples of the ancient forests of the old continental landmass of Gondwanaland, including extensive areas of temperate rainforest.

New Zealanders, I have learnt, do not hike or trek, they 'tramp'. They do not have trails or routes; they have 'tracks'. My intention over the next four months is to 'tramp' at least nine 'tracks', described as 'Great Walks' in the marketing put out by DOC (Kiwi vernacular for the Department of Conservation). Already these words have become part of my everyday vocabulary. With a return air ticket from Auckland scheduled for the end of February, four months from now, I have plenty of time for the nine Great Walks and probably many lesser-known tracks as well.

Full of anticipation, forty Milford Track trampers board the bus in Te Anau. If we hadn't booked months in advance we might have been tempted to cancel the trip; it is bucketing down with precipitation. The bus plunges through driving sheets of heavy rain to Te Anau Downs Harbour, further along the lake. There, what looks like an antique, steam-powered vessel awaits us;

walking out to it on a swaying floating dock, I feel the first twinges of seasickness.

The crew casts off from the bucking pier and the refurbished old boat is tossed on the waves with the liveliness of a cork. Throwing up in the bowels of this boat would likely accelerate a chain reaction among the other queasy passengers, so I escape to the open-sided stern. Rain pours down so heavily that the horizonless view is solid water and it is impossible to tell whether I am gazing at the sky, rain or lake. I am soon decidedly wet, green-around-the-gills and tempted to put on my pack and jump overboard, to hell with the consequences.

'Are we going to tramp the Milford Track or snorkel it?' I wonder aloud, but my not-so-subtle sense of humour is lost on my miserable fellow passengers.

There are two kinds of trampers on the Milford Track: the so-called 'freedom' or independent walkers, and the guided walkers. Each group comprises a maximum of forty trampers, who commence the tramp simultaneously. Accommodation for the two groups on each of the three nights spent on the track is staggered some distance and some hours apart to minimise contact. The poorer freedom walkers, of whom I am one, share large dormitories with bunk beds. We use our own sleeping-bags, cook our own food, bring our own supplies and have no guide. In contrast, the wealthier guided walkers sleep in smaller shared rooms with beds and linen, have shower facilities and are served hot meals in lodges that are considerably bigger and more comfortable than the DOC huts. Of the eighty trampers on the boat, the guided trampers identify themselves by wearing identical yellow rain jackets, with large name tags on the front. Two guides fetch them hot cups of chocolate, trying to coddle their clients out of their collective misery.

Despite expectations to the contrary, our antiquated boat successfully docks at the other end of the lake. The shoreline is thick with vegetation, dripping with rain as if someone up above had pulled the plug. None of those tempting colourful brochures captioned 'the best walk in the world' depicted this saturated scene.

I take my time, stretching and waiting while the other walkers disappear into the forest, like colourful fish sinking into the weeds at the bottom of a murky lake. At the tail end of the group, I deliberately straggle behind. I am eager to begin the track, but I want the intensity of this nature experience undiminished by a chatty fellow tramper. Slipping into the forest, I find it dominated by ancient silver, red and mountain beech trees. The giant trees are soppy with clinging parasitic vegetation, and I touch the moss and glistening ferns with my outstretched hands as I pass by. There is a sense of timelessness, almost a spiritual permanence to this enchanted forest. Long before any of my hairy ancestors were swinging from their branches, these trees, our collective organic lungs, were breathing life into planet earth. Despite, or perhaps because of, the inherent wetness of the rainforest, it is an intense experience.

Hours later, I reach the first DOC hut of the track, the last tramper to arrive. It is no less humid in the hut than outside. Sweaty trampers in long underwear stand in front of lines of gas cookers making dinner. The windows are fogged up with the condensation of a variety of bubbling concoctions. Damp clothes, hung up to dry, steam. The assorted smells of food, boots, socks and sweaty clothes form a noxious mix in the close confines of the hut. The only remaining bunk is tucked tightly under overhead rafters. I pull out my sleeping-bag and unfurl it on the bed before cooking a pasta dinner mixed with a tin of tuna for protein. The mushy paste has the consistency and taste of baby food. Litres of Sleepytime tea compensate for all the perspiration that has poured off me in the walk up here.

Most of us have finished eating when the hut warden enters. He is an older man with droopy eyes, floppy ears and a green DOC sweater, who resembles Yoda out of *Star Wars*. His voice is quiet, almost drowned out by the sounds of water, from the river gushing by the hut and the rain hammering on the tin roof. 'Some of you may have noticed the corner of the hut extends over the bank of the river.' Sure we've noticed, it's a swollen torrent. 'There is a risk the hut could be washed away,' he understates.

Everyone listens intently; he has our undivided attention. I start sidling towards the one door, just in case. 'One hut was swept away in 1989 after similar heavy rains undercut the bank of the river.' His voice is almost a whisper, as if he is required to tell us this but would rather keep it a secret. 'I promise to wake you up if there is any risk of the river undercutting the building.' Then he adds: 'If you hear something during the night, get out quickly.'

With that comforting thought, we go to bed. We have to. The hut warden removes the lantern at ten o'clock and there is nothing else to do. Although I have just lugged my pack some nine kilometres, I am not tired. My mind is a maelstrom of thoughts, mostly to do with the fact that I am doing this trip on my own. After five years sharing my life with someone I love, the sudden adjustment to being single and on the road again is not easy. I find myself brooding, anti-social despite the comforting swirl of conversation as the trampers prepare for bed. I go outside. It has stopped raining and the silhouettes of the mountains are vaguely visible in the clearing cut by the river. The setting is romantic but it makes my bruised heart feel all the more tender. I stroll away from the rushing water, the ambient sounds muted by dense vegetation. Sliding into the dark forest is like entering the dark safety of the womb, where an invisible umbilical cord pumps the forest's life-sustaining nutrients into me. I shuffle along the gravel track, treading carefully in case I should step off its edge into the drainage ditch on either side.

Looking down at my feet, I think I discern stars reflected in a pool of water beside the path. I peer up to confirm this impression, but there is nothing to be seen – I cannot even see through the canopy of trees. Curiosity aroused, I crouch on my hands and knees to examine the pond. I distinguish bluish pinpricks, not a metre from my face, sheltered from heavy globs of falling water by overhanging roots and earth. The mysterious blue sources of light appear to be the eyes of little fairies. I wave one hand towards them to see if they scare, but they stay motionless, unafraid. They are glow-worms, little two-centimetre critters, dangling sticky phosphorescent fishing lines to attract moths. In the silence of the gloomy damp rainforest, the unexpected apparition seems explicable as an assembly of fairies, even if I do know what they really are.

When I return cautiously to the hut, everyone is in bed. I undress and change into a relatively clean and dry set of polypropylene underwear before climbing blindly into my upper bunk. The first snorer begins. An irritated male voice with a heavy Irish accent yells from somewhere: 'By Jesus, will someone not stuff a finger down his throat?' Instead, heavy rain begins to thump loudly against the corrugated tin roof, effectively drowning out the snoring.

During the night, I wake up. There is not a sliver, pinprick or muted shade of light to give any point of reference. It's like being at the bottom of an inkwell in a dark room in the middle of the night. I place my hand in front of my face and touch my flickering eyelashes with my fingertips to make sure my eyes really are open.

I have had too many Sleepytime teas before going to bed and my bladder is bursting. I remain in the cosiness of my sleeping-bag trying to ignore my pressing dilemma. Eventually realising that I had better go out and pee, I sit up – and smack my head hard against the crossbeam supporting the roof. I fall back on the mattress and raise myself again with more caution. I search vainly for my flashlight, which I had tucked under the mattress. It is impossible to see anything without it but I cannot waste more time looking: I'm desperate. I blindly swing my body over the edge of the upper bunk and lower myself slowly overboard, reluctant as a sailor abandoning ship. Feeling with wiggling toes for the wooden frame of the lower bunk, I dangle precariously over the side. The foam mattress, on which I have a firm grip, slowly lifts off the bunk. I fall backwards, crashing into an assortment of packs, the mattress landing on top of me.

The backpacks cushion my fall, but their shoulder straps and waist belts are like a spider's web, and disentangling from them makes me feel like an ungainly insect. I extricate myself, replace the mattress and sleeping-bag and head for the kitchen/eating area, hobbled by tightly crossed legs. Fumbling for the exit, I knock aluminium pots and pans off the kitchen counter. Eventually locating the door, I stumble outside into pouring rain. Not daring to go too far in case I fall over the riverbank undercutting the hut, I uncross my legs and relieve myself into the void beyond the hut steps. It feels a bit like peeing under a cold shower with the lights off.

Thoroughly soaked and cold, I dodder blindly back through the obstacle course of packs, pots and pans. I grope tentatively into what I think is my sleeping-bag and provoke an irate bellow. Dropping back onto the floor, I manoeuvre my way around to another bunk. A probe with my fingertips ascertains that this sleeping-bag, if it is not my own, is at least empty. Scrambling up, I step on the elbow belonging to the occupant of the lower bunk. He curses unintelligibly, staccato Oriental-sounding words flung out at me in the dark.

Amidst the sleeping trampers is a trumpeter doing a solo act. The mother-of-all-snorers is on our trip, although no one except myself seems to have noticed. If the hut were about to fall into the river, Yoda the hut warden would have one hell of a time waking anyone up to warn us.

≥

All our backpacks are lined with heavy, waterproof plastic bags, to keep out the moisture. They have been designed by malicious plastics engineers so that the more surreptitiously one tries to get at the innards of one's pack, the more noise the plastic makes. If Yoda did want to alert everyone of an emergency, the most effective method would be to sneak into the hut and crinkle a backpack's inner lining very carefully and very slowly.

Before dawn my bunkmate takes to sorting through all his belongings, diligently rearranging them in his pack. Not only does he have a big plastic liner bag, but every single item also seems to be individually wrapped in smaller plastic bags. It is impossible to sleep with my lower bunk partner doing the plastic bag shuffle. Frustrated, I sit up and smack my head on the cross-beam again. When I recover, I see, in the first dim light of dawn, that during the night I have turned my sleeping-bag inside out.

It has been snowing in the mountains all night and it is cold. Before we set out in the morning, Yoda tells us: 'The weather forecast is for thunder and hail. With all the snow, you'll have to watch out for avalanches. If you hear a loud crack, something like thunder, it's probably an avalanche; drop your packs and run and hide behind the nearest large tree.' With the weather forecast for thunder, we will be forever dropping our packs and diving for the trees.

With a headache and a noticeably bruised forehead, I'm happy to be out of the noise and confusion of the hut and back into the tranquillity of the rainforest. I hang back at the tail end of the group again. It could not possibly get wetter: I am surprised there is enough air left in the opaque curtain of falling water for us to breathe. Water courses down the muddy path in rivulets, although the track is well maintained, with drainage ditches on either side. My feet slip and slide, my boots and trousers getting caked in mud. If it keeps bucketing down like this, I would prefer tramping with a pair of angler's waders up to the chest. There is more rain here than in Norway, which I have just fled because of its interminable rain and darkness. It rains or snows two hundred days a year in Fiordland. Milford Sound has an annual rainfall of between seven and eight metres, and most of the precipitation is during peak tramping season. The rest of the year it's too frozen to tramp.

A mass of heavy cloud, drizzle and layers of gossamer mist hug the lower slopes of the Clinton River valley. The air is absolutely still, not even the mist stirs. Long lines of waterfall pour magically out of vertical cliff faces. Welts and weeping sores scar the mountainsides, dramatic evidence of past avalanches and waterlogged earthslips. We do not stand a chance. After thunderous false alarms all day, we are sure to be caught out by the real thing.

I pass a boat beside the track, which despite being at least a couple of hundred metres from the river is tied securely to a tree, like Noah's Ark waiting for the flood. Does someone know something we don't? If it carries on raining like this it just might be prudent to hang around the boat for a while and then row downstream.

At midday snowflakes centimetres in diameter invade like miniature parachutes falling to the ground. In the supreme silence of the forest, the Gore-Tex hood pressed against my ears becomes a sound chamber. It amplifies the fall of the heavy snow into dull thumps, which change to sharp rat-a-tat-tats as an artillery barrage of hail pelts my head. If it were remotely possible to raise the white flag and surrender to the elements, I would. Most of the day is spent focusing on my feet, the view visible from under my hood a tunnel-vision of soaked ground. The misty vapour exhaled from my lungs further reduces visibility.

Covered in wet clinging snow, I stagger towards Mintaro Hut. On the way I meet terrorists: half a dozen keas, owl-sized parrots with dark brown–green plumage and bronze-coloured underwings. Imitating me, they stumble along the snowy path, but with the swagger and confidence of professional pirates. They steal anything they can and rip it apart with their lethal, razor-sharp beaks. I leave my baseball cap unattended and within minutes it is shredded and dropped atop a boulder, as if as a kea warning. Another kea attacks my backpack and boots in the short time I enter the hut to find a bunk. Someone else's leather boot, torn apart and unusable, lies abandoned. The tramper must have hopped one-legged over the pass without it. I retrieve my pack and boots before too much damage has been done.

In our group of trampers there are thirty-seven foreigners and three New Zealanders. I approach two of the Kiwis, middle-aged women from Invercargill, and join them in their conversation. They talk about what kind of cars their husbands drive, until I redirect the subject to the Maori legends regarding the origin of rain and mist.

'What Maorri legend might that be?' one asks, rolling her r's like a Scot.

'You know, the one about the creation of the earth and the sky.' They look at me blankly. Having just read about it in my guide-book, the names are still clear in my mind. I explain, paraphrasing the text I have read: 'According to Maori legend, there was noth-ing, not even light, in the beginning. The sky-father, Rangi, lived with the earth-mother, Papa, in total darkness. Their many children – god-of-the-sea, god-of-the-forest, god-of-cultivated food, god-of-wild-plants – didn't want to live in the darkness. They decided to separate their parents, who were preventing light from coming into their world.' The two Kiwi women regard me with the vacant looks of the slightly bewildered. I feel like an authority on the mat-ter compared to my audience. 'All the god-children tried unsuc-cessfully until the god-of-the-forest succeeded in forcing the par-ents apart, and light entered their world. The two parents were very sad they had become separated. Rangi cried so much that much of the land became the sea. Even now, every morning, dew can be seen on the back of Papa, evidence of Rangi's grief. The mist that forms in the mornings in the valleys and rises towards the heavens is Papa's sigh of longing for her husband.'

I like the story, find it touching. Walking in the steep-sided valley of the Clinton River, it is an entirely plausible rationalisa-tion, certainly as coherent as a Christian God creating the world in seven days.

'Ah, don't believe all that Maorri stuff. Load of rrubbish. That's just made up for the tourrists.'

The other Kiwi woman looks sideways at me and says quickly to her friend: 'Ah, I don't know about that.' She changes the topic of conversation to the tourist features of Invercargill.

I vaguely see what looks like a parrotfish staring through the steamed-up window as if it were an aquarium. It's a kea hanging upside down, peering into the room, trying no doubt to get out of the cold and into the mass of belongings inside. Behind the kea the snow falls, flakes so large I can see each one distinctly as it descends through the branches of the trees. The kea gives up try-ing to break in through the window and takes to rolling a stone on the roof, repeatedly fetching it from the gutter and carrying it in its beak to the top to let it tumble noisily down the corrugated tin roof. Since the kea cannot get in, it is vengefully determined to drive us all mad.

The hut is abuzz with excited conversation as trampers talk about the next day and whether we will make it over the pass. Ralph, the third Kiwi in our group, is a mechanic from Kerikeri. He is tall, well-built and good-looking, and has carried several beers up here. He generously offers to share them with me.

'Where're you from?' he asks.

'Canada,' I reply, not telling the entire truth to keep it simple.

'Cool.' He says cool with a hard 'kuh' so it sounds more like 'kuh-ool'. He must be in his early forties; Mandy, his English girlfriend, is half his age. He finds it easier to bond with me than she does, alternately telling lewd jokes or describing his work as a mechanic at an organic orchard. That was where he met Mandy, a nurse, when she was working there as a fruit picker. 'Told my wife I was going to leave her as soon as the kids were old enough to leave home. She never believed me.' He nudges me conspiratorially with his elbow and indicates a group of Aussies sitting huddled together. 'Know why Aussie women wear makeup and perfume?'

'No,' I answer innocently. Mandy grimaces, apparently having heard this one before.

'Because they're ugly and smell bad,' he laughs, as if getting even with the Aussies for their comments about Kiwi chicks. Not sure I get the joke, Ralph adds, 'Know why Aussie blokes don't wear makeup or perfume?' I shake my head. 'Because they're ugly and smell bad but don't know it.'

He has the habit of telling a joke and then laughing at it himself, wagging his chin up and down as if he were trying to rub the chalk marks off a blackboard with his jaw. Over the next hours he imparts his detailed knowledge about what is the best 'new-in-New Zealand' used Japanese car to bring into the country and sell. He has imported one hundred used cars from Japan, purchasing them through a friend who works for Air New Zealand. Why am I so vulnerable to long drawn-out monologues on subjects I'd rather not know about?

When I go outside alone that evening to get some personal space, I try saying 'cool' with a hard 'kuh'. There's a different way of pronouncing 'cool' nowadays: it's definitely more like kuh-ool than cool. When I say 'cool', I sound like an ageing hippie in a drug-induced haze, rather than someone who is really cool, hip and young. I practise and the insulating blanket of snow, which smothers everything with its pale softness, absorbs the sound of my repeated 'cools'.

⇝

Next morning we set off reluctantly under falling blobs of wet, semi-frozen sleet. The upper valley is masked by a much thicker snowy veneer, from which avalanches cascade. We zigzag up to the pass, the snow underfoot becoming deeper, falling continuously in great clinging flakes. As we walk under the trees, clumps of snow slip off branches and fall on us with such regularity it seems as if forest trolls are ambushing us. Fiordland is so like Norway. I found the Norwegian winters impossible, but trolls thrived in that darkness. While the summers were paradise for me, they were lethal for the trolls; a single ray of sun would turn them to stone. They would thrive here all year round.

In several areas, we cross open spaces cleared of trees by previous avalanches. Eventually we reach the bush line, where the trees end and there is nothing to shelter behind. Frequently we hear the noise of what sounds like a jet fighter flying up the valley; an indistinct grumble. Almost as often we locate the avalanche as it tumbles down the mountain. This dull pattern of background rumbles is broken by a resounding crack, louder and more threatening, like the clap of thunder we had been warned about. A cloud of upwelling snow billows as an avalanche cascades down, a semi-fluid river, carrying away everything in its path. It is on the same side of the mountain and frighteningly close to us.

Although we are freedom walkers and therefore theoretically responsible for our own safety, Ruth the DOC hut warden leads the way. A retired and diminutive schoolteacher, she plods through fresh drifts up to our knees and her thighs. Ralph from Kerikeri takes over the lead; being considerably taller than her, he makes faster progress. We are now well above the tree line, over a thousand metres high, which is nothing in terms of mountains, but with these stark alpine weather conditions we could be much higher. There are no points of reference, no cairns, no poles to mark the route. In several places, we wander off the track and fall into deeper snow up to our hips. Finally, we distinguish the vague outline of the stone monument marking the top of the pass.

Ruth stops, almost hidden in the swirling snow. 'The shelter hut is another twenty minutes further up. I have to stay here and wait for eleven other trampers.' The quiver in her voice does not inspire confidence.

Trusting Ruth, we trudge timidly towards the bearing indicated. The snow is deep enough to be difficult to walk through, especially for those at the front breaking the trail. I fall into a crack, snow up to my waist. With my heavy backpack, it takes two others to help pull me out.

'What the hell are we doing here?' one of my rescuers asks. 'Doesn't she realise we're in the middle of a bloody blizzard?'

'I'm not going on, even if she tells us to,' the other replies. 'It's too dangerous and I'm freezing.' No wonder he's freezing, he's wearing running shoes.

We wander around blindly without any real direction, not sure where the path is, nor the shelter we are trying to locate. Ralph leads us, assuming the role of Sir Edmund Hillary II; but Ralph is from Kerikeri in the north part of the North Island, where they do not have anything remotely resembling snow.

It occurs to me to take photographs, as if I have a premonition that something will go wrong and I will need photographic evidence later on. An English girl who immodestly calls herself Amazon Woman is taking reams of film of herself, holding her camera at the end of her long arms. She wears short shorts, what used to be called hot pants, and is so tall she looks as if she is

29

walking on stilts. I photograph her as she takes another satisfying self-portrait.

The storm blows harder and it is difficult to see more than ten metres ahead. The temperature is below freezing, and with the wet snow and the wind-chill factor, some are complaining of the cold. Many trampers only have running shoes and, amazingly, three women besides Amazon Woman are wearing shorts. It seems there is a drop to one side of us, but it is impossible to tell how far. Despite having Kerikeri's own version of Hillary with us, there is no real leadership. Snow collects on our jackets and backpacks, slowly burying us.

Over the previous few summers I had led tourists on ten-day trips into the Norwegian mountains and onto glaciers. Even in summer it would occasionally snow like this. If I were leading a group back in Norway in such conditions, there would be no question of going further, especially with so many ill-equipped, inexperienced people. When Ralph becomes lost and we make a full circle, I tramp back to locate Ruth. She stands immobile, almost impossible to see through the advancing snowstorm, still optimistically waiting for the eleven others to come up the path. I shout into her ear, my voice loud in the eerie silence of the snowstorm: 'Even if we find the shelter, we will never find the way down the other side. Visibility is almost down to zero, the storm is getting worse and several trampers do not have proper equipment for these kinds of conditions. We still have time to turn around now and find our way down.'

'What do I do?' she asks.

'Call them back. They trust you as the leader.'

Blusters of snow engulf us, swirling around Ruth's small face, which is almost hidden under the hood of her jacket. Her lips are drawn tight, blue with cold. 'Can you get them all to come back?' she asks. Her eyes betray fear.

I follow my own trail back to the others. Removing my insulated leather gloves, I shove four fingers under my tongue and whistle loudly. I call out to the group, telling them we are heading down. Amazon Woman relays the message with a lot more authority. She takes one-handed photographs of herself with her other hand cupped around her mouth, calling to the others: 'Come back! Come back!'

Two bearded Swiss men in Gore-Tex, hi-tech walking sticks in both hands probing the snow, head off in the rough direction of the shelter, as does Ralph. They take one direction; he takes another. The rest of us retrace our steps to the monument where Ruth waits. Already the tracks from our ascent have filled with fresh drifts. Within fifteen minutes Ralph and the two Swiss men descend as well. They could barely find their own footsteps; the blowing snow filled in their trail almost immediately.

As we traverse an avalanche area, the steep mountainsides exposed and without tree cover, we meet stragglers from the guided group also returning from an abandoned ascent up to Mackinnon Pass. Together we descend into the protective custody of the dense forest. All of us end up back at Mintaro Hut. Eleven of our group – the ones Ruth kept waiting for – hadn't even bothered to leave. Two Germans are still wrapped up snugly in their sleeping-bags.

It is high season and now there are forty unhappy, name-tagged members of the guided tour sheltering in the hut, in addition to our own group of forty frustrated and tired freedom walkers. Like a factory line, the first arrivals from the next group of freedom walkers arrive up the path from Clinton Forks Hut. Soon there will be one hundred and twenty cold and miserable trampers packed into a hut designed to hold only forty. Yesterday it was crowded and a little claustrophobic. Now it is mayhem.

One of our ill-equipped trampers, a young German, has hypothermia. He is allocated a corner of the hut and two medical students hold his hands. There is a hush, everyone subdued by the seriousness of his condition. Using the hut radio, Ruth calls for two helicopters – an air ambulance and another to haul the rest of us over the pass.

Some hours later, we hear the unmistakable thumping of helicopter blades amplified by the steep-sided mountains. The ferry helicopter nestles onto a raised wooden platform beside the hut; it flits backwards and forwards until evening, evacuating six passengers at a time, starting with the guided walkers. On one flight, the helicopter carries backpacks below it in a swaying sling. Because it is fully loaded, the pilot must execute figures of eight in the narrow valley before gaining enough height to fly over the pass. Between the ferry runs, the medivac chopper arrives with a doctor and a senior DOC staff member from Te Anau. The hypothermic German is transferred to the air ambulance where the doctor hooks him up to monitors. The jet turbines whine louder, the blades rotate and the helicopter takes off, changing the gentle rhythm of falling snow to a gyrating vortex. Then the hovering ferry helicopter takes the ambulance's place on the platform. It loads up again and efficiently disappears into the mountains, which are hidden behind layers of congealed precipitation. It reminds me of an efficient military evacuation, some troops heading to the front, while the wounded are taken to the rear. It must be costing DOC a fortune to bail us out this way and yet there is no mention of charging us for the service.

There are only three of us left when the helicopter comes in for the final run. It is 8.30 and getting dark. Patches of fog and black clouds threatening to dump more snow add a foreboding dimension to the evening. We throw the remaining packs into the vibrating cabin and climb in. The pilot throttles up and backs the helicopter off the pad as if reversing a car out of its parking spot. He flicks the tail around with the foot pedals, and with his left hand gripping the collective and right hand pushing on the control stick between his knees, we head straight for the wall of mountains on the opposite side of the valley. Deliberately giving his last three passengers – a relatively light load – a thrill, he makes us wait for the turn. We are almost into the sheer cliffs before he pulls a steep bank. The flesh of my face sags as I sink into my seat with the gravitational force. We aim for the pass and effortlessly skim over it, then the pilot banks hard right, the helicopter almost on one side before he rights it and descends, hugging the mountain. He flies the machine gracefully, as if it were an extension of his own body. In a cul-de-sac of a valley he banks hard left and cruises in to land, without bothering to hover, outside the guided trampers' Quintin Hut.

By the time we three stragglers arrive at Dumpling Hut, which is further down the track, it is dark and all our fellow freedom trampers have already turned in. Only Amazon Woman is still up, reliving the day's experience in a letter to an ex-boyfriend. It stirs her emotions, and bending my ear she tearfully recounts how she quit her job to join her boyfriend, only to discover he was having an affair with someone else. I hadn't noticed the matching label of LONELY GIRL tattooed on her forehead; amazing how effectively we disguise our afflictions.

Then she asks if I would mind taking a photo of her writing in her diary, several photos in fact, from different angles.

'Just to be sure,' she says, as she tidies her hair and poses, still wearing her hot pants.

The final day walking the Milford Track, the sky is reasonably clear for the first time. The clear weather has brought in a plethora of sightseeing tourists in small aircraft. Walking down to Milford Sound I see a line of nine single-engine planes following one another up the valley, an airborne invasion. Having spent the last few years in Norway, it's a shock to be in similar mountains in New Zealand and experience such an intrusion. That morning I count a total of twenty-seven aircraft passing overhead. With each noisy flight the magic of walking in the primeval forest is diminished.

MILFORD SOUND

It is almost five in the evening at Milford Sound. The horde of tourists has gone back to Queenstown or Te Anau and sightseeing boats no longer dominate the fiord as they had earlier in the afternoon. The terminal building is empty except for a motley group waiting for the motor-sailing yacht and the overnight excursion down Milford Sound. Among them I meet a German couple, Gert and Giselle. He is a neurosurgeon; she has a PhD and works at a pharmaceutical company. They are clearly in love, touching each other frequently. It drives me crazy being in the presence of lovers who are so affectionate; sometimes just the holding of hands can seem like an intimate act. Their public display of affection – PDA – only reinforces my own solitariness.

She asks me: 'Isn't it lonely travelling on your own?'

'Nah,' I reply bravely, although I could break into tears quite easily. I like meeting people, but right now I need my own space to reflect. Time is a magical healing process and walking in these rainforests is the perfect environment for it to do just that. 'I like travelling on my own,' I respond, not telling the whole truth. She looks at me and smiles. She knows I am lying.

We board the vessel and it casts off from the dock. The Sound is dark and grey, the sun effectively blotted out by the overhanging clouds. Within minutes, we see fur seals and then penguins. Enthralled, I stand at the bow with a few others, undeterred by the drizzle. Untamed waterfalls plunge down vertical cliff faces, their spray, despite the massive volume of water, turning to vapour long before the cascading water reaches the sea's surface. It has been raining and snowing heavily for weeks; great swollen gushes of water tumble and slide off the mountains. This is the way nature should be seen. Even the longer Norwegian fiords have nothing on this untamed wilderness.

Giselle and Gert stand silently with me at the bow. The steel-hulled boat hugs the sides of the fiord, sometimes manoeuvring under overhangs, sometimes under the showers of waterfalls. We cruise the fiord's short length to the Tasman Sea, where we ineffectively hoist sail. The vessel thumps into oncoming ocean waves, giant swells which drench those of us still on deck with spumes of salt spray. Finally we turn tail and head back into the sheltered fiord, to cruise under hanging layers of undisturbed mist to calm Harrison Cove, where we anchor. As darkness descends, dinner is served in the mess. The main generator is turned off at eleven.

The setting outside is too spectacular to squander the occasion by sleeping. I climb back to the foredeck and gape down the length of Milford Sound: fold after fold of craggy mountainside against an unruffled backdrop of clouds. Like a black-and-white photographic print pulled prematurely out of developing solution, the ethereal scene has lost all hint of definition, being just an infinite gradation of dull grey. Mountain peaks some two thousand metres above, lit by the leaking light of an obscured full moon, are barely discernible through the mist and cloud.

I feel a presence behind me and turn around to see Giselle. She touches me gently on the shoulder and wishes me good night. Even though she is with Gert, I guess she remembers what it is like to be alone. A small, empathetic gesture like that can mean so much. Although she leaves, it is as if she is still with me.

Exotic sounds burst from the shore, breaking the stillness of the night: moreporks (the native owls), kiwis, kakas, tuis, bellbirds and penguins. The cries echo across the sheltered bay, reverberating from the steep cliff sides. It is not hard to imagine Captain Cook on his sailing vessel, moored silently in this same cove, with the same hidden sounds haunting the ship's crew; or for that matter the Maori on their quests for *pounamu*, greenstone, which they value so much. Little has changed since the forests re-colonised the carved-out glacial valleys after the ice age ten thousand years ago. The glassy fiord is mottled by the tiny silent pinpricks of countless raindrops. I am insignificant in this great moodiness.

I cannot sleep, too many thoughts are rattling around in my head. I climb out of my bunk bed and onto the deck. Giselle is already standing there alone, and I do not disturb her. It is hard to tell when dawn arrives; it is just a different tint of grey. A filmy mist pervades the scene and yet there is no dulling of the senses. It is a world full of magic and portent.

'It is so beautiful, isn't it?' Giselle says, without turning around.

'Yes.'

'It reminds me of Norway.'

'You've been there?' I ask. She had never mentioned this before, although I had talked about living in Norway.

'Yes,' she replies, turning to look at me. 'How long did you live there?'

'Five years.'

'Why did you leave?'

I gaze into the deepest recesses of the fiord, where the union of water and rock face is indistinguishable. 'The long winters in Norway,' I reply, thinking back. 'Not because of the cold, but the darkness and the lack of sunlight . . .' The memory makes me feel cold inside and the still-tender recollections of a concluded relationship do not help, either. 'It's a bit of a cliché, but I know of no better way of describing it: it was as if I was slowly dying, like a wilting plant deprived of sunlight.' Even now it is a pathological fear. I can conjure it at will, the slow descent into darkness as the days become shorter, until they are so perfunctory there is only the barest hint of light even in the middle of the day. 'I couldn't take it any more. I need sunlight. Colour. Unless you experience months of sunlight deprivation, it's hard to explain. With each succeeding winter, it got worse.'

I gaze away from the fiord and at her. 'The summer is different. It's as if nature must pack as much as it can into the two summer months. If winter in Norway was hell frozen over, the summers there were heaven.' It doesn't take much for those wonderful memories to resurface. 'We spent most of the time in the mountains, with a tent and a stove and food. There's no reference point with time; it becomes meaningless when the days are endless. Sometimes we walked until four in the morning and slept until midday. Sometimes we didn't sleep at all.' As much as the memory of the winters fills me with angst, the recollection of the short summers fills my heart with joy. I am quiet, remembering.

Giselle breaks the silence. 'She wouldn't leave?' she guesses.

She considerately looks away again, gazing into the hypnotic distances of the fiord.

'Norwegians are attached to their country,' I reply, as if that was all that was needed to explain the break. There were many other factors: more intuitively than rationally, I had decided the relationship was unworkable. The curt summary is inadequate to describe the anguish of two lovers, wondering whether to cut their losses, wondering whether they were giving up too easily. How does one ever balance that complex equation? I never experienced such depths of loneliness, or such intense moments of happiness, as I did in those years in Norway with Kirsten.

Giselle does not probe any more, allowing me to retreat from the memory.

Kayaks are dropped over the side of the motor-sailor and I paddle away, close to the steep wall of the fiord. I lean completely back, head resting on the rear deck of the kayak, to see the top of Cascade Peak towering twelve hundred metres above. Water somersaults from ledge to ledge of this perpendicular wall of glistening dark bedrock, the whole mountainside an intricate tumbling aquatic lacework. I sit up. A seal rolls over playfully in the water. Three mallards appear out of the mist, swooping in like silent Phantom jets. High-mounted dihedral wings silhouetted against the emptiness behind them, feet lowered like webbed landing gear, they skim to a halt on the burnished water, which is flat as the steel deck of an aircraft carrier. Fugitive layers of mist hover motionless in the impressionistic landscape. I want to absorb it all, keep it somehow within me. I do not take photographs; it would not do the experience justice.

Carried by the momentum of my paddling, I drift through the water. It is impossible not to feel one's heart ache in the midst of this raw silent wilderness. I let my fingers caress the yielding softness of the water, but the gesture is as empty as trying to hold hands with someone who is no longer there.

THE GRAND TRAVERSE: CAPLES–ROUTEBURN TRACKS

It is bucketing with rain again. On their way back to Te Anau, Gert and Giselle drop me off at the Divide, a speck on the map, nothing else besides a shelter. Having waited for hours while the potential avalanches overhanging the road leading up here were pre-emptively 'bombed', I procrastinate even longer to avoid tramping off into the downpour and the rain-soaked forest. I stretch, repack my clothes and watch as busloads of tourists pass on their way to Milford Sound. Most of the jet-lagged Asian tourists are fast asleep, with their heads snapped back, gaping mouths wide open, or foreheads pressed flat against the windows.

A DOC utility vehicle pulls up to the shelter, the driver with a crew cut, a long fringe and an ear riddled with at least a dozen earrings. I recognise him as the warden from Dumpling Hut on the Milford Track. He introduces me to a man with Rastafarian dreadlocks, the warden from Lake Howden Hut on the Routeburn Track.

'What are you doing here?' I ask the Dumpling Hut warden.

'It's my days off, so I thought I'd do some tramping and visit my friend.'

Are these DOC hut wardens for real? They work for a living in isolated huts and when they get time off they go for a walk in the bush. They make me look like a socialite.

The Rasta carries a hunting rifle with telescopic sights. The two men have wicked glints in their eyes, giving them a decidedly degenerate appearance. Their weird hairdos don't help either. I'm not sure whether they are deliberately trying to look like inbred Appalachians, or whether it comes to them naturally.

'You two look like you're straight out of *Deliverance*,' I comment, sealing my pack against the rain with the outer cover pulled tight over it. 'What's the rifle for?'

'To hunt down punters like you who haven't paid their DOC hut fees,' the Rasta taunts. He flicks his dreadlocks out of his face, suddenly taking on a more sinister appearance.

'Seriously,' I reply.

'Hunt introduced species.'

'Like deer?' I suggest.

'Like tourists,' the other answers.

'Sure beats talking to them,' the Rasta laughs, throwing the rifle over his shoulder. He fingers a box full of ammunition.

'We'll give you a couple of hours head start,' continues the Dumpling Hut warden.

'Very funny.' I swing the backpack onto my back and slope off, with just the occasional apprehensive glance over my shoulder. They wouldn't really do that, would they?

They yell after me: 'Any introduced species not on a farm is noxious. You don't need a licence to shoot them!'

I quicken my pace. These tracks are not on farmland, and as a tourist I am after all an exotic species, along with whitetail, red, fallow, wapiti and chamois deer, pigs, goats, possums, rats and stoats. Even the brown and rainbow trout are introduced. Once again under the reassuring influence of the forest, the mild terror inspired by the jokes abates. There is no mistaking the overwhelming sentiment of wellbeing, as if my physical body instinctively understands that without these trees, we could not live.

The Caples Track, not listed as one of the Great Walks, diverts off the Greenstone Track. The first ominous sign is a collapsed footbridge half submerged in a stream. The path is overgrown and doesn't look as if anyone has used it. I trudge through mud and water calf-deep. My boots and socks are already soaking wet – and I am only just starting the walk. I have to climb over fallen tree trunks, or crawl under them, and wade semi-immersed through flooded streams. It is more like an SAS obstacle course, designed to break the spirit of the unfit and unqualified. And why not? This is a wilderness, after all. I have been spoilt by tramping the groomed Milford Track.

I struggle up a steeply ascending trail that is often not a path at all, it's so riddled with twisted roots, loose stones and tangled branches. Water gushes down, rendering the ground as slippery as a waterslide. I am dripping with perspiration and cannot believe I am doing this for fun. A sapling bent back to its full extent thwacks me on the ear and I trip, skewering my hand on a thin stump. I will self-destruct trying to complete this walk; the two hut wardens won't even have to hunt me down. Years from now, when DOC decide to elevate the Caples track to a 'Great Walk', they will find a skeleton pinned under a heavy green rucksack. A handwritten note in my bony fingers will bequeath my wealth, most of which will have rotted on my back.

Despite this scenario, to my amazement I successfully reach the top of the pass. To my even greater surprise I find myself traipsing with ridiculous ease along a boardwalk covered with chicken wire, winding through patches of heavy snow. Even if I tried, I could not slip on the horizontal planks – I could walk on them blindfolded. A sign warns not to step off the path, which has been constructed to protect the delicate ecosystem.

In contrast to the ascent, the walk down the other side of the pass is pleasant, dominated by beautiful, naturally sculptured green rocks. Soon I have descended out of the snow. Water jostles gently down a series of rock-lined waterfalls into pools fringed by ferns. The trickling waters of the creek are clear, with a seemingly jade hue, the impression soft and ethereal, as if painted with the washed-out strokes of an ink brush. It all looks suspiciously like a contrived, ornate and rather extravagant Japanese garden.

At Upper Caples Hut, my footsteps thump heavily across the wooden porch. I take off my muddy boots and enter. Four young Kiwis, two girls and two boys, mind their own business, playing cards. I could make the effort to initiate a conversation, but I am too exhausted to be bothered.

Two young American trampers arrive. They break the ice and talk to the four card-playing Kiwis, who all prove to be dental students from Dunedin. I listen to the conversation about American talk shows. The future dentists brag about watching all of them: 'If one is on when we have classes, we tape it and look at it later. It's unbelievable what Americans do and say on television.' Their tone is disparaging, as if religiously watching such rubbish was no reflection on them.

When I reach Lower Caples Hut the next day, it starts snowing and raining. Although it is only mid-afternoon, I am exhausted from yesterday's effort. I light the coal-burning pot-bellied stove, retreat into my Norwegian sleeping-bag and catch up on back issues of *Reader's Digest*. The most recent copy is twenty years old. It thunders and hails outside but I'm snug as a bug in a rug. Drowsy with oxygen deprivation from the burning fire, I fall asleep with a *Reader's Digest* over my face. At dusk the hut warden wakes me to ask for my hut pass. I am the only tramper and he invites me to join him and his female companion, an off-duty hut warden from the Routeburn Track, for home-brewed beer. Several hours later, full of good cheer, freshly shot and stewed rabbit, and a growing respect for the generosity and hospitality of Kiwis, I stumble back into the trampers' half of the hut.

≈

The Routeburn Track brochure states, in its 'Winter Dangers' section: 'The benched track above Lake Harris becomes a dangerous steep slope crossed by avalanche paths. Deep snowdrifts cover the Hollyford Face. The zigzag above Lake MacKenzie freezes and becomes covered in ice . . . Avalanches can occur between Earland Falls and Routeburn Falls. The risk is highest in late winter and spring, after heavy rain or snow.'

Great. I'm here in spring, with the heaviest rain and snow for decades. Makes for exciting tramping. I should have brought crampons and an ice pick with me. And a helmet too.

Walking with rain and snow entirely obscuring the views for which the Routeburn track is famous, I have nothing better to do than practise saying out loud a laconic 'Ah yeah,' in the Kiwi accent. All day, as I walk through rainforest and climb the dangerously icy steep slopes crossed by avalanche paths, I chant 'Ah yeah,' repeatedly to myself like a mantra. I change the inflection in my voice, the pronunciation, the tone and the timbre. Sometimes I almost sound like a Kiwi for several 'Ah yeahs' in a row and then suddenly I lose it again, saying 'Ah yeh,' or 'Ah yuh,' or 'Ah yah,' or even 'Ah ye.'

At Harris Saddle I eat a picnic lunch consisting mostly of chocolate bars. While being dumped on by heavy snowfall, I hold conversations with myself, designed to give as many reasons to respond, 'Ah yeah,' as is socially possible. A few more days travelling alone like this and I will be a babbling idiot. Any eavesdroppers would have reached that conclusion already.

Members of a fluorescent-clad Japanese family pass me by as I munch on a third chocolate bar. They lean into the wind while shielding their faces from pelting hailstones. Their private Kiwi guide leads them, her radio cackling. There are two classes of trampers on the Routeburn, just like the Milford, except here they can walk in both directions. The young son of the family stops to talk to me, determinedly practising his English. Pretending to be a cool Kiwi, I reply with sufficiently close approximations of 'Ah yeah,' to his numerous questions. He continues asking me questions, thinking I am the genuine article. Trouble is, I can't say anything else in Kiwi, so I answer all his questions, no matter what, even if it's the wrong answer, with 'Ah yeah.' He finally gives up and scurries through the hail after his family.

I zigzag down the icy hillside, through snow-covered dense rainforest as thick as I have seen anywhere in New Zealand. Lower down, nearer Lake MacKenzie, amidst the verdant undergrowth where shrubs, lianas and ferns drip on the forest floor, I am the only thing that is not a shade of brilliant green. Small creeks and seepages are smothered with flourishing layers of mosses, lichens, liverworts and filmy ferns, nurturing a damp underworld where fairies surely must thrive. The cushion of greenery absorbs the sounds of nearby waterfalls.

When I reach Lake MacKenzie hut, the warden asks me for my pass.

'You're English aren't you?' I ask.

'Naw I'm not. I'm a Kiwi.'

'Ah yeah,' I manage to say, phonetically successful for once. 'Since when?'

'Ah yeah, four years ago?' He has that distinctive Kiwi upward inflection at the end of each sentence, but seems to be exaggerating it. At least he has the off-hand 'Ah yeah,' down pat, which is more than I can say for myself, despite practising it all day.

'Ah yuh, you sure picked up the accent fast,' I say, flubbing the 'yeah'.

'I've worked at it so the Kiwis don't pick on me for being loopy,' he admits.

'Loopy?' I repeat, sounding like a North American. He does not look loopy to me.

'Loopy means a foreigner. Like you,' he says smugly.

KEPLER TRACK

Back in Te Anau and after a day's rest, I bound around the lake. It's a breezy clear day and I'm feeling good about the physical process of tackling another track. That's one good thing about tramping for hours every day: I'm so tired, I fall asleep each night despite the thoughts stuck in my head, like the frayed strands of a thread jammed in the eye of a needle. The sound of waves lapping rhythmically on the stony beach reminds me of camping on the shores of lakes in northern Ontario, but the ringing calls of unfamiliar birds render the experience exotic. On the far side of the lake I climb up a wide path carpeted with the delicate brown leaves of beech trees, native conifers like the rimu, which grows as high as sixty metres, miro and kamahai. I stop to watch a tiny bird, a male rifleman, as it chases a female: they dodge in and out of the hanging vines and bearded moss, around tree trunks and through the ferns. Further up the path, the thick bush does not peter out but ends suddenly at over one thousand metres above sea level, in open meadows of tawny tussock grasses covered in a layer of snow.

While I am making dinner in Mount Luxmore Hut on the Kepler Track, Eisaku, a young Japanese, offers me a sushi roll: rice with crunchy salmon skin inside. He sits with me and talks.

'I have been studying in Auckland for eight months. Now I am tramping around New Zealand.' He is pensive. 'Yeah,' he adds with a perfect Kiwi inflection. 'I want to stay here. Maybe find a job. Here, is very nice for me. I like New Zealand.'

Eisaku conforms to the stereotypical workaholic image of the Japanese by diligently going through a book full of algebra problems. 'Good fun!' he says. They are indecipherable hieroglyphics as far as I am concerned. I unsuccessfully tackle a problem, much to his amusement.

Outside, it is snowing heavily.

It must have snowed all night. Several centimetres of fresh snow cover the ground. This is not what I had expected when I migrated from the northern hemisphere's upcoming winter to New Zealand's summer. Although there are enough warnings about the variable weather in the mountains, many of the backpacking-through-Asia-and-Australasia crowd hardly seem equipped for these conditions. The hut warden, another retired teacher, advises those outfitted only with running shoes, jeans and small daypacks to retreat to Te Anau. Others stay in the hut to wait it out for another day.

I elect to go on, perhaps even thankful that the others will not be crowding the track. Eisaku asks if he can join me as far as the next hut and I lend him an extra pair of gloves and a woollen hat. I am happy to include him with me, for the safety factor. We climb the exposed ridges for which this track is well known. The route is snow-covered, and in places it has collected into deep drifts. In good weather, the Kepler Track provides spectacular views on either side but now it is bitterly cold with a howling windstorm. We are well above the tree line, with nothing to protect us from the blast of the wind. At fifteen hundred metres, where a narrow saddle joins two peaks with steep drops down icy slopes, the gusts are strong enough to knock me off balance, despite the weight of the heavy hundred-litre backpack.

Visibility is negligible. I deliberately slow down, taking my time breaking through the fresh snow, making sure Eisaku is always within sight, only a short distance behind me. We trudge through knee and thigh-deep ice-cream curls hanging over the ridgeline, following the faint traces of the track indistinctly marked by the protruding tips of steel rods. The wind accelerates, thumping against the hood of my Gore-Tex jacket. The waterproof cover for my external-frame backpack flaps even louder, like a mainsail in a gale-force wind. I can hear little else. The track twists and turns, rising and falling with the regularity of a roller-coaster ride, and the wind blowing in our faces reinforces the comparison. It demands our respect until we descend through the tree line back into the protection of the forest.

At Iris Burns Hut, the tall bearded hut warden booms at us: 'Clean up after yerselves in the morning. I'm not yer bloody mother.' He gives each of us the evil eye. The other trampers in the hut have come the other way, up the valley and have yet to go over the exposed palisades of the Keplers. 'This morning I had to run after a bunch of Israelis who left their rubbish here. Caught them at Rainbow Reach.' He looks fiercely around the room. It will be spotless in the morning judging by the faces avoiding his stare; nobody wants him loping after us with our forgotten rubbish. He leaves it to our imagination what he did to the Israelis. Turning to Eisaku and me, he says: 'You two were a bit of a worry; lucky to make it over the top. Full on up there, mates. Was talking to Mount Luxmore Hut on the radio at three this afternoon and only just able to hear them. Blizzard conditions. Worst spring weather we've had in over a decade.'

And that, in Fiordland, says a lot.

≶

Next morning I eagerly extract myself from the warmth of my sleeping-bag and wash my face in icy-cold water. Although I enjoy pitting myself against demanding weather conditions, it would be nice to have a view of the surrounding mountains. The

45

weather is better than yesterday – the cloud cover is above the mountain peaks. Rather than continue on the track down the valley, I decide to go back over the ridges. Crazy as it may seem, I want to see the Keplers again on a clearer day.

Eisaku decides to complete the circuit. He gives me a gift of Japanese food, instructing me how to cook it. His last words are: 'Please, you must be very careful.' They ring in my ears for some time after I set off happily on my own. The patches of clear blue sky reveal fresh snowdrifts and pristine white peaks arching over the ridges, like ocean rollers flash-frozen at the crest just before they collapse. When the sun shines, it is as if millions of diamonds have been left scattered on the bed of fresh snow. If I could, I'd collect them all for a rainy day.

The trek seems to take forever and my tummy growls with hunger. I fantasise about a dinner of lamb chops, *kumara* (sweet potatoes) and corn on the cob, with a dessert of chocolate and ice cream. I can see Te Anau below, corrugated roofs shining prettily amidst the rivers snaking across the glacial delta. I am so hungry I can almost smell the food in the restaurants. Of course, if I was in a real rush to stuff myself with food, I could always pump up my biceps and return to the pub with the special sammies.

'Are you the guy who stomped out of here in a huff last time?' the barmaid would enquire, before wrapping me in a wrestler's lock. I am faint with hunger and that bit of horseplay would probably finish me off.

On the way down through the forest I meet Yoda the hut warden from the Milford Track. 'What are you doing here?' I ask, snapping out of my nightmarish daydreams.

His ears flop alarmingly. They look as if the tops are made of wax and are melting; if they droop much more they'll surely fall off. He replies: 'It's my days off, so I thought I would tramp around the Keplers.'

Another one. Don't the DOC wardens have a life? They live in isolated huts for a living and then traipse alone through forests for fun? They take the Lonely Guy concept to extremes. I secretly watch him as he tramps up the track. What's going on in that head of his? What's going on in mine?

At Te Anau I head straight for the supermarket, lumbered with my backpack. I spend my last fifty dollars buying half a dozen lamb chops, sweet potato, corn and a few other goodies. I have not eaten since last night and have walked more than twenty kilometres today.

I rush to the backpackers giddy with greed, but when I unpack the shopping bags in the communal kitchen, I discover that half the food I bought is missing, including the chops. I have heavy jugs of orange juice and milk, but they will not fill the rumbling cavities inside me. I run back to the supermarket and frantically tell the cashier: 'I must have left a bag full of groceries here just fifteen minutes ago.' The bag is nowhere in sight and she calls the manager.

'Do you have your receipt?' the manager asks calmly.

I urgently give her the tiny piece of paper.

'Do you know what you are missing?' I nod. 'Follow me.' She proceeds to collect the missing items, with me following her up and down the aisles. 'Chops this big?' she asks, wafting a package under my nose, with several bloody, juicy red chops easily visible through the cellophane. I nod and drool, like a bedraggled dog that has not been fed by its master for a day. 'Better to err on the plus side,' she says benevolently. I agree enthusiastically, wagging my tail. In the vegie aisle, I catch a glimpse of myself in a mirror and realise I have a vintage tramper-head. I try to fluff and reposition my hair into a shape resembling a human head rather than a deflated rugby ball.

She hands me the full grocery bag beyond the cashier, so that I do not have to pay for it. My intestines feel like they are tied in a knot: I don't think I've ever been this hungry in my life. If I'm not careful, I'm going to keel over. I don't want to delay the process of tucking into this feast, but I don't want her to think that I'm ungrateful either.

I wipe the saliva from the corners of my mouth and ask: 'How can you run a business if you give free bags of food to absent-minded shoppers?'

'Nah,' she says. 'Whoever was behind you took your bag by mistake. Happens all the time. We just replace the food that's missing. They'll bring it back.'

If I had accidentally found myself with an extra bag of free groceries I would rationalise that it was divine intervention and keep it. 'I know who was behind me. A big Maori guy.'

'He'll bring it back,' she replies. 'It was an honest mistake.'

I thank her profusely as she ushers me out. She says: 'Good as gold.'

'What?'

'Good as gold.' She sees the look of incomprehension on my face. 'Means OK. No problem.'

Tightly clutching the good-as-gold groceries to my chest, I scurry back to the backpackers. I dump the bags on the counter, turn on the stove, put some garlic butter in the pan and start cooking, cutting off pieces of baby sheep ribs to eat even as they fry. There is no smooching. There is no foreplay. This is the gastronomic equivalent of an instant orgasm.

Lying prone in bed, still in post-orgasmic bliss, I read the *Southland Times,* gently resting the paper on a full belly that looks as if it could be a few months pregnant.

TRAMPER DIES AFTER FALL FROM TRACK
A three-day friendship between two tourists ended in tragedy yesterday when one of them, a Canadian, died in a tramping accident.

The story goes on to explain in detail how the two had been out in the same awful weather as Eisaku and I. The Canadian had slipped down an icy slope. I reflect that had I not been with Eisaku during the climb that day, I probably wouldn't have walked as slowly as I had, waiting for him to catch up. There were plenty of slippery slopes to have fallen down, too.

STEWART ISLAND

Isolated at the southern tip of the South Island, or 'the Mainland' as South Islanders prefer to call their half of the country, is the settlement of Invercargill. There is a certain indefinable charm to the town, despite its main Dee Street being a gauntlet of fast-food joints, 'new-in-NZ' used-car lots and toys-for-boys farm machinery. Maybe the appeal has more to do with the people who live here and their down-to-earth friendliness. I don't even have to stick my thumb out to hitch before someone stops to offer me a ride. You couldn't meet more hospitable people. Perhaps it's because 'The World's Southernmost McDonald's' is Invercargill's most obvious claim to fame and the burghers are over-compensating.

Waiting at the airport for the weather to clear before the short hop across the Foveaux Strait to Stewart Island, I flip idly through the *Southland Times*. The front page has a photograph of an English publican who is walking from Invercargill all the way up to Cape Reinga at the top of the North Island. Unlike me, he will literally walk every step of the way, on roads and highways. Curious to see what someone who walks the length of New Zealand would look like, I scrutinise the photo carefully. Why would he want to see New Zealand from the perspective of a highway shoulder?

On page two, the crime report lists several offences occurring in the past twenty-four hours:

- A first-aid kit was taken from a car.
- A rose in a terracotta pot was stolen from a grave at the Eastern Cemetery between Thursday and Saturday.
- Five poppy plants were removed from a Bamborough Street property.
- A half packet of cigarettes was taken from a bar in Tweed Street.
- A pair of glasses was taken from a Thames Street house.
- A forty-litre petrol tin was taken from a farm at Awarua Bay.

• A man was hit over the head with a No 9 frozen chicken needing six stitches.

There is no clarification as to whether it was the chicken or the man needing the stitches.

This crime wave is given prominence, but the deaths of locals are allocated less column space. I read with alarm that: 'The reign of terror which led to the deaths of at least three kiwis on Stewart Island ended on Saturday when two dogs were destroyed. Since then no further kiwis have been found dead.' I'm not so sure now that I want to visit an island that places so little importance on the death of its citizens.

My flight is announced and I am swept along with a bunch of stalwart Stewart Islanders returning from a shopping spree to the 'mainland'. Still nervous, I point out the 'reign of terror' article to the Kiwi sitting next to me on the plane. 'Ah yeah,' he comments, leaning towards me confidentially. 'Kiwis can't fly.' The comment does not inspire confidence. I stare down the centre aisle and watch as the pilots flick switches on and off and fiddle around with the paraphernalia to be found in any aircraft cockpit. I hope these Kiwis can fly.

The dilapidated twin-engine Islander sags under its full load, horrifying creaks and groans hinting at metal fatigue. Like a crippled moth, it taxis the huge expanse of runway, which is almost as wide and long as Dee Street. The aircraft does not immediately lurch forward when the captain pushes the twin throttles to maximum thrust. It slowly picks up speed and momentum, and at the end of the long runway it lifts hesitantly into the air, defying all proven laws of gravity. The plane banks ponderously over the grid-patterned concrete and asphalt of this urban outpost, the endless green pasture encompassing the town mown to resemble golf fairways by a sizeable portion of New Zealand's seventy million sheep. Then we flutter out over the frigid waters of Foveaux Strait. The aircraft's navigational equipment had better work: if we miss Stewart Island, the next stop is Antarctica.

The view out of the window on our port side reveals a foreboding black cloudy sky with zero visibility. By contrast, on the starboard side, the sun shines brightly, sparkling off the waters below and lending the scene a holiday atmosphere. The clouds drift east, away from Stewart Island. Within twenty minutes we are floating against the wind over Halfmoon Bay, above bush the colour and apparent density of giant heads of broccoli. A tiny postage-stamp sized clearing carved out of the bush is the landing strip.

I pray that the brakes and reverse thrust of the props function properly and we don't crash into the trees at the end of the dirt runway. To distract myself, I study a brochure of the island but surreptitiously cross my fingers underneath the pages. I read how William Stewart, an officer of the sealing vessel *Pegasus*, compiled the first detailed charts of the southern coast of New Zealand. In a fit of modesty, he named the third-largest island in New Zealand after himself. It hangs almost forgotten off the bottom of the South Island, like the dot of an exclamation mark. Captain Cook, exploring the area on his earlier tour of duty, had mistaken the island for a peninsula, forgivable for someone who navigated the world with a hand-held sextant, a prototype chronometer and no Global Positioning Satellite.

In Maori legend, New Zealand's islands are more imaginatively named. According to the legend, the demigod Maui, who lived in Hawaiki, went out fishing with his brothers. He dropped his magic fishhook over the side of the canoe and caught a great flat fish, which became the North Island. The South Island was Maui's canoe, and Stewart Island was Te Punga o te Waka a Maui, the anchor stone.

Landing, the aircraft groans, moans, creaks and squeaks in protest at the rough ground. The ground crew, meaning someone nearby on the airstrip, opens the door to the cabin and a bewildering cacophony of unidentified birdsong greets us, as if we had just been emptied out into an aviary. The air is noticeably fresh and clean, laced with the fragrance of vegetation and flowers. The temperature is cool, the chilly wind blowing down the runway. Walking from the airstrip towards the settlement, I keep a sharp lookout for Kiwi-eating dogs. I trust they can tell the difference between a Kiwi and a Canuck far from home; I should have stitched a maple-leaf flag prominently on my pack.

In the Department of Conservation office in Halfmoon Bay, I ask how dangerous it is to walk in the rainforest.

The DOC worker answers: 'There's nothing dangerous here, except a spider and that hasn't been seen for a while anyway. Niver iver bite you.' She converts the 'a' to an 'e', the 'e' to an 'i' and the 'a' in front of an 'r' to a double 'aa', dropping the 'r', as in cars to 'caas' and farms to 'faams'.

'What about those dogs?'

'You mean the dogs that killed the kiwis?' she says nonchalantly.

I nod, trying to look cool about the subject too.

'Destroyed them.'

'So I should be safe?' I ask, just to be sure.

'They attacked kiwis,' she explains.

'But how did they know the difference?'

'Between what?'

'Well, like between me and a Kiwi.'

'Between you and a kiwi?' she repeats.

I nod.

She blinks a couple of times, then with the infinite patience of a civil servant, launches into a spiel on the native wildlife. 'Pre-human New Zealand was separated from other land masses in the Mesozoic period, more than 150 million years ago, before the evolution of land mammals. The only native mammals in New Zealand were two species of bat. That's why birds became the dominant fauna. Some bird life adapted in the absence of mammalian predators to become flightless or weakly flying birds, like the kiwi.'

'You mean kiwis can't fly?' I repeat my fellow passenger's assertion.

'Yeah. That's why it's so easy for the dogs to get them. The other birds can fly out of danger.'

The penny drops. It seems incredible that over the tens of millions of years some mammals, apart from bats, did not find their way to these fertile islands. None of those odd and dangerous creatures from Australia ever climbed on a piece of wood and drifted across the Tasman Sea. There are no snakes of any kind here, never mind poisonous ones. Apart from humans, there is nothing to eat me, maul me, trample me, bite me or even scare me to death. Even the dogs are going to leave me alone as long as I don't flap my arms helplessly.

I continue through the settlement. Outside a wooden cottage with a white picket fence, a hand-painted sign proclaims it to be 'Jo and Andy's Place', in competition with 'Ann's Place' and 'Dave's Place' down the road. Jo and Andy's place proves a little austere, heated by coal and wood, and with a chemical toilet. Yet it is connected to the real world and Jo's mother by e-mail umbilical cord. Both Jo and Andy have fled the moral decay of America and this is about as far as they could get.

Halfmoon Bay was first settled in 1865. The first post office opened soon after in 1872 and the first school in 1874. There is a frontier-style general store, an old pub and a few quaint wooden cottages barely protruding from the thick vegetation, smoke curling from their hidden chimneys. A dozen fishing boats rock lazily at their moorings on glassy, breathing swells; sea birds strut self-importantly on an empty beach. It definitely feels as if I am far away from anywhere: there is no one in sight. I pass an empty bowling green, a Returned Servicemen's Association hall, and an Anglican church. The only sign of life is the pub, which has a couple of battered cars parked outside. Where do the owners of these cars drive? There's nowhere to go.

Were it not for the simple memorial to the soldiers who died in the Great War, the peaceful cove would seem totally removed from the rest of the world. Of the one hundred thousand Kiwi troops sent to fight, seventeen thousand were killed and another forty-one thousand wounded. The names of several brave local boys are inscribed on the stone monument.

I stride along a narrow, winding asphalt road leading to the start of the Rakiura Track. Rakiura, I read somewhere, is the Maori name for Stewart Island. Unfamiliar birds are everywhere, including a black bird with an iridescent shine on its back and twin blobs of white feathers like wattles hanging under its throat. I stop to listen. Its voice is almost, but not quite, melodious, fluid chimes followed by an assortment of harsher notes, clonks, chuckles, squeaks, clucks and clicks. It sounds drunk. I stop, unload my pack from my shoulders and seek out my bird book. Inevitably it is at the bottom of the pack, and by the time I successfully extract it the scene looks as if there has been a traffic accident: clothes, plastic bags of food, stoves, pots, pans and a sleeping-bag are scattered on the empty road. Thankfully there isn't any traffic. I look the creature up and discover it is a tui, New Zealand's national bird.

I divert off the narrow lane skirting idyllic coves, to shuffle my feet on sandy beaches, sucking in salt air pungent with the odour of rotting seaweed. Waves wash over the beach. White daisies and garlic flowers, thick patches of gorse and broom sprout like weeds beside the road. I cross over a headland thick with bush, past the decaying remains of a sawmill. The tallest trees are rimu, a red pine, but there are also kamahi, thin-barked totara and southern rata, providing a canopy of foliage up to twenty metres high. Ground ferns, tree ferns, vines, perching orchids and moss completely blanket the enormous trunks; there is such a profusion of burgeoning parasitic vegetation that it is often impossible to identify the trees underneath. Grass trees and lancewood saturate the middle layers; clumps of gahnia tussock fill the spaces at ground level. Dense colonies of crown fern and taller wheki tree fern fronds pack the gaps. At the bottom level are bush lilies and a variety of orchids. A stinkwood tree proves, when I squeeze its leaves, fetid. I hear the raucous cries of what I think is a parrot, then see several bronze-coloured kakas swooping heavily through the bush. They resemble the alpine keas. One lands clumsily on a tree trunk and roughly rips off the bark with its beak as it searches for grubs.

Through a gap in the bush, I see the sun reflecting off water in a bay fronted by an expanse of dark sand. The sound of surging surf beckons as I descend to Magnetic Beach. The sea is placid, its swells curling over in a long line to wash upon the shore. I dodge waves fanning over the exposed sand, which is littered with seashells. Stiff-legged wading birds strut along the beach; black swans, beaked bows facing into the breeze, resemble an anchored fleet of galleons.

A DOC hut is tucked in among a stand of tall eucalyptus trees. I rub my shoulders where my pack has hung like a lead weight and pull out a map. The Maori had a semi-permanent hunting settlement here, despite the inherent loneliness of this place. I stare out at the dense bush, the empty cold ocean. I imagine the sealers, the first whites to shelter in the bay in the early nineteenth century. The whalers, who came and made it a base in the mid-1850s, remained here for a year at a time, processing whale blubber before heading back to Europe. What was it like for these men isolated in this remote corner of the world, so far from home?

When gold was found in a creek in the middle of Magnetic Beach in 1867, the first resident police station had to be established to maintain law and order among the unruly miners. Later the New Zealand government subsidised the immigration of Shetland Islanders, but even the stalwart Shetlanders found it too desolate a place. This secluded bay might be designated Port William, but it is deserted; it is impossible to detect prior evidence of human settlement. Apart from a jetty and the DOC hut, there is nothing in this forlorn place but bush.

Walking along the beach, I discover empty shells of scallop, mussel and abalone (paua), bull kelp, kelp bubbles, sea urchins and a dead porcupine fish. I sift through all this natural flotsam and find not a scrap of discarded plastic, shred of netting or shard of broken glass. On the tide-exposed rocks and beach, I collect a pot full of cockles, mussels and oysters, then find a fist-sized octopus clinging to rocks just under the water line. I pluck him out and dump him unceremoniously in an aluminium pot with the rest of my dinner.

As I watch the sunset, a weka, a flightless brown bird resembling a hen, walks within easy reach. His mate follows, pursued by two chicks, all of them unconcerned by my presence. The adults communicate by a curious drum-like sound. One of the wekas pecks at the eyes of my boots.

Rakiura translates as the 'land of the glowing skies', and the island lives up to the name with a burning sunset. I bask in the last rays, almost off the edge of the world, further south than I have ever been before. Stewart Island is further south than South Africa, closer to the South Pole than Tasmania, almost on a par with the Falkland Islands. It is about as far as you can go to hide without getting ridiculous. This is, after all, only New Zealand.

As dawn breaks in the forest, birdsong precludes sleep, as if someone has turned the stereo up; but with the sunrise the racket fades. Waking up alone here seems perfectly OK; in this setting, there is no stigma attached to being single. Being solitary enhances the experience, or so I persuade myself. With no incentive to stay in bed, I swing out of the top bunk and stuff my belongings into my backpack. Then I zigzag along the beach before slipping into forests haunted by the sounds of unseen birds.

I have this primeval urge at the end of each autumn, before winter sets in, to migrate to greener pastures, richer hunting grounds, as if to stay too long in one place would invite discovery from enemy tribes. There must be some genetic truth to this restlessness; a reason why my European ancestors thousands or even tens of thousands of years ago survived. My ancient instincts for survival compel me to move on – I cannot fight them. Resisting these impulses creates turmoil; giving in to these urges keeps me in balance with myself. I am often told how lucky I am to embark on these journeys. It is not so much a matter of luck as a matter of choice. But there are drawbacks to this incessant life of wandering; I have no tribe to bond with, no family of my own to provide a familiar sense of belonging.

There is something mystical about walking alone through forests. Although this one has been milled in the past, huge rimu and rata trees stand testimony to what the virgin podocarp forest must once have looked like. The sun cuts through the foliage, casting light on the ground in shimmering splotches of browns and greens, like a turtle's shell. The shadows stir with the canopy above, swaying in the blustery breeze. Massive tree trunks chafe together with the ominous heavy creak of a wooden sailing ship rolling in heavy seas. The snorted warning of an unseen deer startles me. I take some photographs, but they can hardly do this velvety rainforest justice. I forget trying to capture the scene with my camera and concentrate on experiencing this thriving nature. I commit to memory a stand of crown fern back-lit by the sun, an iridescent lime-green kaleidoscope thrust out of a sombre, indistinct underworld.

The luxuriant forest is primordial, a perception enhanced by the haunting chimes of the invisible bellbirds and tui, the raucous cries of the kakas and red-crowned parakeets. It is easy to imagine spirits in the forest watching my every move. A plump New Zealand pigeon balances heavily above on a tree branch. The bird is disproportionately fat; like a bumblebee, it hardly seems capable of flying.

At the tops of ridges, where the higher ground collects more rainfall, everything is smothered in a fuzzy thick carpet of ground ferns: drooping spleenworts, filmy, chain and hound's tongue ferns. It is impossible to see the forest floor, or the branches or trunks of trees. From the perspective of the aircraft, the forest below had looked impenetrably thick, uniform and intimidating. But from within the forest it is surprisingly open, yet with a sense of intimacy and femininity. My heart heaves, with a passion far more profound than I could have imagined. Alone in the midst of this vibrant rainforest, I feel a sensuality of being that borders on erotic.

I lower my pack to the ground and sit beside a stream stained rusty by tannin. Removing my boots and socks, I dangle my feet in the cool current. There is nothing to fear. Lying in the prolific vegetation, my face to the side, nose close to the ground, I breathe deeply. If I could, I would bottle the moist fragrance of the New Zealand rainforest so that I might open it later and recall the essence of these feelings. Eerie sounds of unseen bellbirds ring magically from somewhere deep in the forest, echoing my enchantment.

≈

I wait by the wharf for the catamaran ferry service back to the South Island. A hefty woman in a lumberjack's jacket stomps around the office.

She barks at me in a strong Kiwi accent: 'Throwyourpeckin-thetubouthebeckthire.'

I cannot comprehend what she is saying. I ask her to repeat it, but still cannot understand. 'Sorry, could you say that just one more time?'

The woman looks skyward and swaggers out in a huff. She crashes the forklift truck around the dock for a bit, as if dispelling her frustrations with the foreign punter.

A woman in the waiting room says, in a more understandable accent: 'Don't worry about Kathy, she gets like that sometimes.'

As we cross the straits between Stewart Island and Bluff, the port serving Invercargill, huge swells thrust the boat forward like a surfboard on the crest of an infinite series of waves. The catamaran skitters about as the force of the surge lifts us from behind. At the open back of the boat, diesel fumes eddy around us, making me nauseous. Kathy the lumberjack-turned-sailor busily stomps around the deck throwing coils into ropes.

I timidly ask: 'Do you have any anti-seasick pills on board?'

'In the cabin on the right-hand side, there's a first-aid box with a plastic bottle. Take a couple of those. They work fast.'

Funny how I can understand her now. 'I hope so,' I reply, with the deliberate threat of puking over her clean boat. She actually smiles for the first time. I stumble into the cabin, which immediately makes me feel sicker, locate the first-aid box and grab the plastic bottle. Instead of two pills, I take three for good measure, replace the bottle, and emerge onto the deck. Maybe if I keep my eyes focused on the horizon . . . I wait for the pills to take effect, but I feel worse rather than better.

'How're you going?' Kathy asks, still smiling. Her thick legs balance against the pitch and roll of the boat like a tree trunk, while I am thrown about the deck like a loose cannon.

'I feel like I'm going to puke,' I reply. This is not an idle threat.

That changes her demeanour. 'Take another pill. That should definitely do it. Works for everyone else,' she adds.

If she really cared, she would get me the pills herself. I lurch below deck again, swallow another two pills, and quickly resurface. I wait for the medicine to take effect but there don't seem to be any curative effects from these particular seasick pills. Maybe it's too late. The boat is pitching about crazily as we enter shallower water and I'm not sure if I'm going to make it. I am surprised Kathy hasn't handed me a seasick bag, in which case she could have the best of both worlds: watch me puke and not have to clean up.

'How you going, mate?' she asks, with fake concern.

'Worse,' I tell her. This is definitely going to be touch and go.

'You're sure you took the right pills?'

What does she take me for, an idiot? 'Of course I'm sure.'

'Works a charm for everyone else. Which pills did you take?'

'The ones you told me to take. In the plastic bottle in the first-aid box,' I reply, getting peeved. She should just leave me alone to die in peace.

'Show me the bottle,' she says disbelievingly.

She's asking for it.

I stumble below and fetch the unmarked plastic bottle, tempted to swallow another pill or two. I emerge and thrust the container at her. 'Here, take a look for yourself.' I can taste the vomit in my breath. It's there, just ready to go.

She takes the bottle out of my hand and studies it incredulously. 'That's not the bottle of anti-seasick pills. That's just aspirin. No wonder you're feeling awful. Look, there's no label on this bottle,' she says slowly, as if speaking to a dimwit. 'The bottle of seasick pills is clearly marked . . .'

I lean against the rails and puke, aiming for the surf, but the strong swirling tail wind blows my breakfast back into my face. I smear the remnants of half-digested porridge into my beard like a decidedly unseaworthy version of Roald Dahl's Mr Twit. Kathy puts a heavy hand on my back to make sure I remain facing the frothy whitecaps.

At least I don't have a headache.

≈

I disembark from the catamaran with decidedly unsteady legs and a queasy stomach. Despite being in no shape to hitchhike, I am barely onto the road with my thumb tentatively stuck out before a black Holden sedan skids to a halt beside me. I study my thumb with amazement. The Holden has darkened windows, fat low-profile tyres, and what looks vaguely like a gurgling chrome toilet seat sticking out of the bonnet. The jacked-up rear-end of the car growls and sputters outrageously. I cram my pack into the back before climbing into the fleece-covered bucket seat, where I sit as if embraced by a convulsing sheep in its death-throes. The driver is so young he barely has peach-fuzz gracing his upper lip. I doubt if he has ever shaved. This quivering mobile steel contraption is his mechanical steed, his throbbing pride and joy, his proof of rites of passage. A pair of fluffy dice dance from the rear-view mirror as we shudder off the shoulder, kicking up a rooster-tail of gravel. We accelerate down Dee Street a lot faster than the twin-engine Islander airplane had managed at take-off. This time it is the Holden defying the law of gravity by remaining on the ground.

We soon find ourselves behind a police car with flashing lights, following two halves of a house, each dwarfing a low-bed tractor-trailer. The concept of 'home-delivery' is given a whole new meaning. We vibrate impatiently behind the house before we finally pass with a squeal of tyres and a rumble like thunder. My stomach is mimicking the furry dice dancing from the mirror and just when I think I am getting used to the Mad Max ride, I puke violently into my lap. Vomit puddles into the sheepskin under my groin. The driver pulls over to let me off.

Abandoned in the middle of nowhere, I clean up as best I can. A Good Samaritan soon pulls up alongside, dressed in white from head to toe. He opens the boot of his car automatically from the driver's seat and I hoist my pack inside. When I jump into the front seat he says: 'Never do that. If I had been a Bad Man, I could have driven off with your pack.'

'Well, if I had been a Suspicious Man, I could have taken your Car Licence Number as you drove off and then I would have told the Police.'

'True.'

He relates the minutest details of his life story to the accompaniment of proselytising gospel tunes on the tape deck. I try to ignore the smell of my crotch. My next ride is from a tired but gigantic sheep shearer who says absolutely nothing, not a word, but plays the same gospel as the Good Samaritan. We pass someone with a backpack walking on the shoulder of the road, head down. I guess it is the Englishman on his way up to Cape Reinga. Contrary to my expectations, he looks perfectly sane.

I am dropped off on the outskirts of a small settlement, but before I can stick my thumb out again, the air brakes of a double tractor-trailer snort and gasp. It pulls over on the shoulder, engulfing me in a cloud of dust. The driver jumps out of the cab wearing an oversized baggy jumper and apparently not much else over bare legs. I am apprehensive about his intentions until he helps lift my pack into the interior of the trailer, revealing a tiny pair of stubbies, rugby shorts.

An hour later he lets me out at a fork in the road. A driver stops his car to ask if I would be interested in delivering his sedan to Christchurch. 'I'll pay the petrol and you can take two or three days to deliver it if you wanted.' I decline, as I'm not heading back to Christchurch just yet, but I have to wonder at the trusting nature of these people. Within minutes, another ride picks me up.

I could be tempted to settle in this hospitable, bucolic corner tucked away from the rest of the world. Even while I talk with the driver, I cannot take my eyes off the spectacle of a world so incredibly pure and unspoiled. I want to saturate my senses with the feel of this peaceful place. The sparse, small frontier settlements of rectangular bungalows on either side of the road do not have the charm of old European villages and towns, but they are clean, appear safe and fit the clichéd description of New Zealand. It is like an innocent Midwest North America, or Britain – at a stretch of the imagination – fifty years ago. A man walking his dog waves as we drive by. I smile and wave back, as though I knew him.

A little old lady stops to give me a ride. Like the rest, she asks how I like New Zealand and when I respond positively she invites me home for tea in Te Anau. After pavlova – meringue with fruit and cream piled on top – she drives me to a backpackers lodge. I walk to the supermarket under low-slung black clouds threatening to rain or snow, and ask the manager if the grocery bag I mislaid a couple of weeks ago was ever returned. She remembers me and smiles. 'Ah yeah, we got it back. The person behind you brought it in. No worries.'

At a pub that night, I recognise the tall muscular Maori, nodding in time to the beat of the local band. 'You were the guy who was behind me in the supermarket a couple of weeks ago,' I yell over the awful noise blasting out of speakers the size of a vertically mounted DOC bunk bed. 'I think you accidentally took one of my bags of groceries.' He barely notices me. 'Thanks for taking the bag back,' I bleat, looking up at him.

He glances down at my earnest upturned face. 'No dramas, mate,' he says. He seems unsure why I would bother to thank him for his honesty, which is normal here, even if it isn't in the rest of the world. As we watch the band render their barely recognisable imitation of a Beatles song, he says: 'Going off in here tonight.'

'Yuh, you can say that again,' I reply, flubbing the 'yeah' yet again. I shrug my shoulders in approximate time to the tune, attempting to look cool, like one of the boys. The music is more than just going off though, it's rancid.

'Yeah, choice group,' he adds, totally confusing me.

DECEMBER

≈

QUEENSTOWN – WANAKA – GREYMOUTH – CHRISTCHURCH

'*Cool*,' the young Scot replies, when I tell him I am headed for Queenstown. 'So are we. Throw your pack in the back seat.'

I crawl in beside my pack, which takes up most of the room. 'Queenstown is fantastic,' he adds, as we continue down the highway. His girlfriend sits up front with him. They look like teenagers, although he must be at least twenty. Must be their sun-protected complexions with all the rain back home. In New Zealand everyone looks older than they really are. Must be the sun and the hole in the ozone layer.

'That's where they invented bungee jumping,' he continues with enthusiasm. 'Cool place. You can do anything there. Go bungee jumping off the biggest jumps, go on jet-boat rides, dirt biking, parachuting, paragliding, river-boarding, skydiving, hang-gliding, kayaking, canoeing, horse riding. Full-on place.' He uses the Kiwi vernacular, having picked it up, he tells me, during the six months they have been driving around the country in their Holden. 'Tried to get a job in Queenstown but everyone wants a job there. Queenstown has it all. Ever been bungee jumping?' he asks, lighting up a cigarette. I have to concentrate to understand his broad Scottish dialect.

Distracted, I reply, 'Uh-uh.' I continue to admire the perfect scenery, while sticking my nose out the open side window to get a whiff of fresh air. It doesn't get much more picturesque than this anywhere in the world.

'You should. You'd like it.' His head bobs in synchrony to the radio tunes. 'It's cool.'

'Actually, I would like it about as much as I would enjoy dodging highway traffic during rush hour. Not a lot of skill involved in having someone tie a giant rubber band around your ankles and push you off a big drop.' I can be such an amenable guy but sometimes little twerps like this start wagging my tongue for me.

'Tried parachuting then?' he asks, undeterred.

'BTDT,' I reply dismissively.

'What?' he asks.

'Been there, done that.'

'How about jet boating?' he persists.

'Too wilderness intrusive,' I respond. The jet boat, invented in New Zealand, is unique in that it dispenses with propellers. Unfortunately, the impellers built into the hull provide powered boats with shallower draft. Practical as that may be, it gives jet boats greater access up otherwise non-navigable rivers, into what would normally be impenetrable wilderness regions. Great when you are trying to 'tame' the bush, but not so great when you are trying to conserve it.

'Should try rafting then. That's not wilderness intrusive.'

'I used to own a rafting company in Norway, on the Sjoa River.' That's also about as beautiful a setting as you could ever hope to find. I'd be hard put to choose between the Sjoa and here for scenic beauty.

'You don't any more?'

'Every time there was a drowning, the bookings went up. Didn't like the mentality of the clients. Bunch of yahoos.' At his age I was rafting and doing a lot more foolish things too.

'You had drownings?' He turns around, eyes wide, as if this were an inconceivable consequence of rafting.

'Every summer.' At least he is quiet after that. I stare out the window at the landscape. To compensate for my testiness, I fill his car up with petrol when we get to Queenstown. I love the enthusiasm of younger travellers; their lives are in front of them and they're excited about everything. I hate it when I start acting and talking like a killjoy.

Queenstown is the kind of party place that fills up on Friday and Saturday nights and empties just as quickly on Sundays. Arriving on a relatively subdued Sunday afternoon, I walk up to the gondola on the mountain overlooking the town. Despite the beautiful setting, the 'full-on' tourism of Queenstown has destroyed whatever authentic New Zealand atmosphere there might once have been. The commercialism has little appeal for me, despite the build-up given by the Scottish couple during the drive up here. With all the businesses vying for the tourists' dollars I can't help but feel uncomfortably like a punter, and I decide to continue on to Wanaka tomorrow.

A casualty from the party weekend walks up the path at a snail's pace in front of me. As I pass, I stop practising saying 'cool' with a hard 'kuh' and ask her: 'What's there to do in Queenstown?'

'I don't know,' she says. 'I arrived here on Friday night to party, and this is the first time I've been outside since then.' Although she is young, she has dark rings under her eyes. 'Still got a hangover,' she adds proudly.

She has what I detect is a Scandinavian intonation. Sometimes I amaze myself at how quickly I can recognise foreign accents. Often I can guess within a couple of spoken words

'Kuh-ool,' I say. 'You're Danish, right?'

'Canadian,' she replies.

❧

The Wanaka backpackers lodge reflects the tone of this settlement, which is downright sleepy compared to Queenstown. Befitting the more laid-back atmosphere of the place, classical music plays softly as backpackers play chess or read. I set off early in the morning for Mount Roy, which towers solitary on the other side of the lake. In a setting like this, it is impossible not to fantasise what it would be like to live here permanently. I could easily be tempted to settle in Wanaka, a community in a setting as beautiful as Queenstown's, but still unspoilt by mass tourism and rabid urban development.

From the summit of Mount Roy, I peer through my camera at panoramic views of tiny sheep in green fields, a turquoise-blue lake and snow-clad mountains. By twisting the polarised filter to punch out the sky and paint the lake a darker blue, I can saturate the colours by removing the extraneous reflections.

It takes me most of the day to walk all the way around the lake to the top of Mount Roy and back to the backpackers. My mind is full of thoughts, memories triggered by the cool air and the scenery. The hike reminds me of walking in the mountains of Norway some months ago. On my last day in Norway and our last day together, Kirsten and I walked up a familiar valley, well above the tree line. It was one of those rare September days, the weather stable, the sky blue; although it was cold, the sun was strong enough to warm us in its direct light.

Already the grass and bracken had turned rusty autumn colours. We both knew that this time tomorrow, I would be gone. I wanted to climb one last peak. With the intensity of the condemned we hiked to the summit, where we sat huddled together staring out over the surrounding mountains and valleys. Only the fading September sun kept us warm. As it dropped in the sky, the shadows crept up the hillsides. Then the sun disappeared behind the mountains, casting us in its shadow. Once again, the familiar deep-rooted fear of an impending Norwegian winter cast its icy tentacles into the depths of my being.

I held Kirsten tightly, knowing that tomorrow I would not be able to hold her any more. As I scrunched up my eyes, the tears I had successfully been holding back squeezed out, dampening her hair. She started crying too, great hulking sobs. The sound carried far down the valley.

In the morning, when I roll up to pay for the overnight accommodation, the owner of the backpackers says: 'You look terrible. You going to travel feeling like that?'

I nod. It's hard to know if am really sick or whether I'm just so psychologically down that I feel like an invalid. LONELY GUY is emblazoned on my forehead again – and I don't have a sense of humour about it today.

'God loves a trier,' she says, shaking her head.

I sleep on the bus most of the way to Franz Josef Glacier on the West Coast. I have a burning fever, my joints hurt, and it feels as if my eyeballs are being pushed out of their sockets. It could be psychosomatic, but I am sweating despite feeling cold and shivering uncontrollably. Everyone avoids me as if I had the plague, just when I could do with some TLC. I have a cold, probably the flu, but I worry this may be a recurring bout of malaria. I had planned to walk up the glacier as soon as we arrived in Franz Josef but I feel too sick to manage that. The idea of a glacier extending down through rainforest almost to sea level had seemed incredibly appealing when I read about it. But now all I want to do is get into bed.

At a hostel in Franz Josef, most of the backpackers sit hypnotised in front of a television, watching *Seinfeld*. Why come all this way and then watch TV shows from home? The owners of the hostel must love the television. Keeps their clients nice and docile. I watch for a few minutes and find myself even more alienated from my fellow humans. Never having owned a television, I find it hard to understand these sitcoms. Sometimes I think I must be a Martian, unable to relate to a vast component of earthlings' lives. I feel as strongly about television as I do about recreational drugs. It can be such a waste of human lives, especially young ones. I catch myself again, being crabby, antisocial, although it can hardly be social to sit with a bunch of uncommunicative backpackers watching television. I crash on a bed and dejectedly study the poem pasted on the back of the bedroom door.

Hostel Life

Well, I've roamed the world, over many a day,
And a hostel's the place I generally stay.
Now there's some things about them that's always the same,
It's a world-wide conspiracy, that's what I claim.
'Cause there's always one who stays out till three,
Then turns on the lights 'cause he cannot see.
He smells like a pub, and he's usually drunk,
And he steps on your arm when he climbs in his bunk.
And then there's the one who leaves pots in the sink,
And when they run out, it's your milk that they drink.
They sprawl on the sofas so there's nowhere to sit.
Consideration? Hell, they don't give a . . . !
And the worst ones of all, they're really a drag,
Keep every bloody item in a different plastic bag.
Now I've spoken with others, and they all feel the same,
We're all considerate and we are not to blame.
So who is this group which disrupts hostel life?
Who stirs us from dreams and causes such strife?
Now I'm not paranoid, but it's a thought that I've had,
They're all on the payrolls of our mums and our dads.
They follow us around wherever we roam,
Making life miserable so we will all go home.
But the last laugh's on our loved ones,
And that is for sure,
Because as for the travel bug,
There is no real cure.
They can torment us and tease us,
But when all's said and done,
In spite of it all, we're still having fun.

Cathy '90
BC, Canada

I feel sick. And empty. And I'm not having fun at all.

I labour down the road to catch the bus to Greymouth, my back-pack seeming heavier than ever. A team of sightseeing helicopters circle noisily overhead, carting passengers to the glacier and back. ATVs (All Terrain Vehicles) bounce away full of tourists and a light plane takes off with skis attached to its wheels. The

68

Franz Josef village is a staging point for an army of tourists on manoeuvres.

I had really looked forward to climbing on this glacier. For five years I took groups of people up the glaciers in Norway. The magic of the glaciers was awesome, without intrusive sounds. All you could hear was the trickling of meltwater, the crunching of crampons on granular ice and the occasional almighty crack as a piece of glacier moved or dropped. No ATVs, planes or helicopters distracted from the intensity of the nature experience.

In the bushes by the main road is a hut decorated with hobnailed boots, iron cooking utensils and initials carved into bunk beds and walls. This museum was the original shelter, now transplanted, where visitors overnighted when they walked through the forest to reach the foot of the glacier, which they climbed with ropes and crampons. Remarks in the visitor's book reflect the awe and fascination that early tourists had for the glacier. It is cheapened now; it's almost a fabricated Disney World. Witnessing this magical and spectacular experience rendered mundane by modern technology leaves me with an even emptier feeling.

The bus arrives. I climb aboard to be confronted by a stocky woman in slacks and a brooch with 'IYQ' in big gold letters pinned to her blouse. She smiles at me and says loudly: 'Hi!'

I look at her as if she were a toad belching. I ask: 'IYQ?' and fall into her conversational trap.

'You do? Well IYQ too and so does Jesus,' she replies, in a southern United States drawl. She sits down next to me and insists on talking, especially when the driver speaks over the intercom to impart information.

'Could you repeat what you just said?' she asks him. Even before he has repeated it for her sole benefit, she is already asking me: 'So, where do you come from?'

Don't these types ever stop to listen? I tell her: 'Yi yam from Peru,' pretending I cannot speak or understand English.

We hurtle down an empty ribbon of road pressed to the sea by mist-shrouded mountains. I rest my head passively against the windowpane as New Zealand streaks by. A helicopter has landed in a paddock, blades still rotating, the pilot in a jump suit taking a leak. On the other side of the helicopter, two hunters stack the floppy carcasses of magnificent red deer stags into the back of a utility truck. The sight depresses me.

I am having a bad day and accept it as such. I have to learn that not every day can be a high.

Greymouth was a hive of activity during the gold rush. Now its main industries are coal mining, fishing, sphagnum-moss collecting, farming and tourism. A huge man with a walrus moustache and a beer belly talks with several others, all festooned with long scraggly beards. If they had tried to look like goldminers from the last century, they could not have succeeded better. The town, despite its unprepossessing name, is authentically colourful.

The train to Christchurch is delayed, so I ask a woman walking by: 'Could you tell me how far it is to the nearest supermarket?'

'It's a five-minute walk that way,' the woman replies, pointing down the road.

I follow her directions, and half an hour later I am still on my way to the supermarket. It is not the first time a helpful Kiwi's assessment of how long it takes to walk somewhere is out of whack. I don't think they've ever actually strolled these distances: the supermarket is a five-minute drive and a forty-minute walk.

On the wobbling little narrow-gauge train to Christchurch, the conductor holds up a camera: 'Does this belong to anyone?'

'It's my Nikon,' I say, when he sashays close enough for me to recognise it.

He hands me the camera. 'You left it on the platform. Someone found it and handed it in to the ticket station.'

Kiwis tell stories of how New Zealand is not as crime free as it used to be, that now you cannot park your car in a parking lot at one of the hiking tracks without having it broken into. My own experience has been truer to the cliché: that old-fashioned New Zealand is as honest and naïve as North America was a couple of generations ago.

The train wiggles its way through mountains and dense forest, affording an occasional glimpse of snow-capped peaks and long stretches of open, bouldered rivers. Dense mist steams out of the thick vegetation like smoke. On the other side of the pass is a deluge of heavy rain. I am very happy I decided not to get off en route to take on another waterlogged track.

AKAROA

Arriving back in Christchurch for the second time, I am more aware of the town's distinctive appeal – for one thing, I can see the sun. I join a walking tour and recognise quaint scenes depicted in coffee-table books. Our guide, a retired schoolteacher, leads us into Christ Church Cathedral and proudly points out a stone plaque dedicated to the memory of one of the original 'Canterbury Pilgrims', who arrived in 1850. She pulls her frame up to its full diminutive size and says: 'I was fifteen years old when that original pioneer died.' The anecdote puts the short history of New Zealand in perspective. Even the Maori, in their giant canoes, arrived in these islands from Polynesia as recently as a thousand years ago, which is nothing compared to the Australian Aborigines' claim to be the oldest living culture at fifty thousand years. The Maori named their new homeland Aotearoa: the land of the long white cloud.

I look forward to starting another track, hopefully one not thoroughly soaked with rain and snow. In the late afternoon, I step aboard the Akaroa shuttle bus.

The driver greets me: 'How you going, mate?'

I show him the brochure. 'I'm about to do the track across the farmers' fields.'

'Your name Stevenson?' I nod. 'Well, somehow they've cocked that up. Got you booked on the wrong track. It's going to be a bit of a case sorting that one out.'

He starts the engine. There are no other passengers.

'Is there a big difference?'

'They copied ours.'

'Ours?'

'Yeah. I'm one of the owners of the land that the track goes through. The other track people phoned me up to see if you were coming on the four o'clock shuttle. If so, I was to drop you off at the church in Little River.'

'Can I get on your track still?' I want the original, not a copy.

'Sure, but you'd better sort it out with them first.' He smiles as he puts the bus into gear.

We drive out of Christchurch towards the volcanic hills to the south-east. All the instruments, dials and instructions on the bus are in Japanese. A 'new-in-NZ' used bus.

'How's your Japanese?' I ask the driver. 'I mean, how do you know what knob does what? Everything's in Japanese.'

He looks at the dashboard. 'Tell you the truth, I don't. My wife usually drives this bus. I'm a farmer.'

'Your wife can speak Japanese?'

He laughs.

I am dropped off at the church in Little River. The church door is open and I walk in. A woman vacuuming the carpet sees me, turns the machine off and smiles radiantly. 'Andrew!' I smile and nod encouragement. 'We were expecting you at one.'

'Well,' I say, pleased that someone should actually know who I am, 'I think there's been a mistake. You see, I was in Te Anau when I booked and they didn't know that there are two tracks around here.' I am prepared to walk this one even if it is a copy, all things being equal. 'Have the other trampers already started?'

'There are no other trampers.'

Bad sign. I was hoping to break out of my solitary routine and tramp with a group of others. 'Would it be terribly disappointing if I cancelled?' The thought of doing another track on my own has lost the appeal it had weeks ago.

She almost looks relieved. 'No problem.' They are not going to charge me a cancellation fee. 'What are you going to do instead?' she asks.

'See if I can still get on the other track. Is there a phone here?'

She points. 'There's a phone booth in the village, that way.' She packs up her vacuum cleaner, then asks: 'By the way, when did you find out about being on the wrong track?'

'On the bus on the way over here,' I answer, not appreciating the internecine politics of competing private tracks.

'Ah yeah, well I sussed that one out correctly,' she says abruptly. The smile gone, she ushers me out of the church like a chicken out of the coop.

I walk the few hundred metres to the phone booth, look up the telephone number on the brochure and dial. When a man answers, I explain: 'I was in Te Anau about two weeks ago and thought I'd booked a four-day trip on your track. Unfortunately, I've just discovered that there are two similar tracks here, and the travel agency booked me on the wrong one. I'm in Little River now and they don't mind if I cancel. Do you have an opening for the four-day track, starting this evening?'

'No worries, mate, we've got room for one more.'

'I'd like to sort out the payment situation first, though. I've already paid the full amount to the travel agency. I'm sure that when I phone to explain, it'll be no sweat for them to transfer the payment to your outfit instead.'

'No problem, just get yourself over here, mate. We can sort it out.' He sounds like another easy-going, laid-back Kiwi bloke. 'You're going to miss the shuttle bus to the first hut, leaves Akaroa at six sharp. But I can send a taxi down to get you for twenty bucks.'

'Thanks, that's very thoughtful of you.' I look at my watch. 'I might make the bus; I'll start hitchhiking now.'

As soon as I stick my thumb out, a red van stops. The driver gets out to help me hoist my pack in, and when I explain my predicament, he accelerates. It is a few minutes past six when we arrive in Akaroa, just as the shuttle bus is about to pull away. I scramble out of the van into the bus, to be driven the very short distance to the first hut, which is situated on the sloping curve of a hill, overlooking the harbour. The exorbitant offer of a twenty-dollar taxi ride must have included an open bar in the back seat.

Arriving at the hut, I discover that the rest of the group is comprised almost entirely of Kiwis. Perfect, a chance to mix with the locals. I find myself a room with a couple of empty bunk beds. The man on the phone's line about there being only one place left was either wishful thinking or a good marketing ploy.

Not yet fully recovered from the flu or recurring malaria or heartache or whatever it is I am suffering from, I put my sleeping-bag on a sofa on the covered porch and crawl into it. I hear the pop of champagne bottles inside. One of the Kiwis comes out to ask: 'Would you like to have tea with us? There's heaps of food.'

I'd definitely like to get to know these Kiwis, but I don't feel up to it right now. There will be lots of time as we do the track together, staying in the same huts each night. 'Lost my appetite, but thanks anyway. Maybe tomorrow.'

They sit down to eat. A loud English woman dominates the conversation. She is celebrating her new Kiwi citizenship and I overhear her mocking the formal ceremony, in which she swore allegiance. The story is told as if the whole thing had been a bit of a lark: she ridicules herself and the ceremony. She tells how there was also a family of five Vietnamese at the ceremony, and I wonder if the Vietnamese family's reaction to finding a new home, so peaceful and tranquil compared to their war-torn country, was as flippant as her own.

I ignore the conversation and study a pair of nesting swallows with baby chicks just above my head. The parents twitter around busily as the sun drifts lower over the surrounding hills. We are perched on the edge of a gradient overlooking the filled-in caldera of an ancient volcano and the open sea, surrounded by green fields. The setting could not be more bucolic.

Over the Kiwis' conversation, I hear what sounds like a dirt motorbike without a muffler approaching. A man steps noisily on the covered wooden porch into the hut and says 'G'day!' to everyone. 'I'm the owner of this hut,' he announces. Then he asks: 'Is there some single foreigner here?' They point in my direction. He sees me lying in my sleeping-bag on the porch and struts up, reaching a hand out. At first, I think he is extending it in greeting and reach out in return. But he is not extending a hand-shake. 'I need $120 off you,' he demands.

His jeans are ripped, his sweater is shredded in several places, he is covered in grime and his hair is uncombed. Even backpackers do not look as threadbare as this guy. He reminds me of a cartoon character after a stick of dynamite has accidentally exploded in its hands. He keeps his upturned palm extended, waiting for me to fill it with dollars.

I shift to an upright position, uncomfortable talking to him while lying prone in my sleeping-bag. 'As I explained to you on the phone, I've already paid. I'd like to get the payment I made to the other track transferred to you.'

'I don't care what you've got to do. It's nothing to do with me.' He has an unmistakably aggressive look about him. 'I don't want a fight with you.' He spits out the word 'fight', spraying phlegm onto my upturned face.

Who is asking for a fight? I am lying helpless in a sleeping-bag feeling sicker than a dog. This cartoon character has come out of the forest beating his chest, defining his territory. What happened to the nice bloke I talked to on the phone, who was so under-standing, calling me 'mate', telling me *we* could work out the payment? I do not feel like a tourist with a minor problem that can easily be sorted out in the morning with the management. Either this wild man should be on stage, or locked up. 'Look, I think I'll just quietly slip out of here and resolve the finances in the morn-ing,' I say meekly, as I extricate myself from the bag.

'How are you going to get to Akaroa?' he asks.

'I'll walk.' It is now past sunset and almost dark. I drape the sleeping-bag over my shoulder and head to the bunkroom to col-lect the rest of my gear.

Then, out of the blue, he offers me a bit of advice. 'There's a backpackers hut a hundred metres up the hill. You can see the smoke coming out the chimney. They have a vacancy.'

The Kiwis are all silent. The farmer mumbles derogatory asides: 'Bloody foreigners are taking over the country.' With my tail between my legs, I walk up to the backpackers lodge in darkness.

A pleasant Swiss manager shows me the 'cabins', outside the farmhouse. The physical setting is lovely but the 'cabins' are the most dilapidated, hillbilly structures I've seen anywhere. I say to the manager, 'Back in Canada, you would not be able to get a permit to operate something like this. Could you do this in Switzerland?'

'No, I'd be in jail.' It is the only time he says no. The rest of the time he says: 'Yeah, yeah, yeah, yeah.' He looks like a ventriloquist's dummy. I opt for the cabin that looks least likely to collapse on top of me in the middle of the night. When I follow the manager back to the main farm building to retrieve my backpack, in the gloom I see my adversary sitting on a sofa glowering at me through blood-shot red eyes.

'Is this your place as well?' I ask, nervously grabbing my pack.

'Yeah.'

Fuck.

CHRISTCHURCH —KAIKOURA—NELSON

As I start to hitchhike again, a woman stops to pick me up almost before my thumb is out. She is barefoot, with close-cropped hair and a broad smile. 'Shove your pack in the back,' she says, opening the tailgate of the station wagon, which is filled with pillows and futons and clothes, all tossed about. I pitch the pack in with a practised motion, landing it neatly on a futon.

I tell her about the incident with the farmer. 'Doesn't surprise me,' she commiserates. 'Picked up a hitchhiker, a girl, and she was still so upset with her reception there she started crying when she told me what happened to her.'

I don't want to go on about this negative experience so I ask her: 'What about you? Where are you from?'

She tells me about herself as we drive to Christchurch.

'I was born in Gore, inland and north of Invercargill, and moved to Christchurch when I was still a child. When I was fourteen I met a Maori from Akaroa. At sixteen I married him and had my first child. Both my children are at university now, and I'm divorced. I did my big "OE", you know, our Overseas Experience? During my seven months in London I became a Buddhist and a Shiatsu therapist. I loved it there; I could be whoever I wanted to be, totally anonymous. No one cared what I did. When I came back to Christchurch, I almost left again. It seemed so conservative and small-minded. I felt stifled. I cried myself to sleep that first night back; it was such a flat, empty feeling. I had changed so much, but none of my friends had, so it was hard to relate to them. Christchurch seemed so quiet compared to London. That was a few years ago.'

'Has it changed since then?'

'A lot, especially in the last three years. It's becoming more cosmopolitan. Attitudes are changing fast among the pakeha.'

'Pakeha?'

'Whites. I'm glad I decided to stay in New Zealand now, but for a while I wasn't. Too many guys with the attitude you just encountered.' She is silent for a while as we drive through the rolling countryside. 'Now I'm taking courses in the Maori language.'

'But you're no longer married to a Maori?'

'Always been interested in Maori culture, even before I met my husband. I love the Maori legends, their songs, stories, dance. Maoridom captivates me.' She gets animated as she talks. 'It's strange because I feel like a Maori, even if I'm not. When my husband and I divorced, I was upset that my ties to Maoridom might be cut, but then I discovered I had Maori relations, a great-uncle in Bluff. That made me happy, really happy, like I had Maori blood in me. It explained why I identified so much with the Maori people. I felt a Maori after all, and proud of it. But when I went to visit my relatives in Bluff, I found out my great-uncle was Spanish, not Maori. Then I had a real identity crisis.' She nods, remembering. 'I explained my affinity for everything Maori through having a Maori relation, and when I discovered I wasn't a Maori at all, it kind of pulled the carpet out from under my feet.

I became withdrawn, depressed.' She is quiet as we drive through impressive farmland.

'And then I figured: this land is of the Maori. They've been here for over a thousand years. I too am of this land, born and bred, therefore I've got Maori in me too. That's good enough, whether there are blood ties or not.' She turns to look at me. 'Then I was happy again. I could understand my identification with the Maori culture and history. It's all a part of this land called New Zealand and I'm a New Zealander.'

I like that story.

She drops me off at a backpackers lodge in Christchurch, where I find myself with an Irish roommate who has spent the last three weeks in New Zealand. He has official 'Government of New Zealand' papers spread all over his bed.

'Jesus, if I'd known it was going to be so cold, I wouldn't have come here,' he says, pulling on a jumper. He has been travelling around on a backpackers bus, but bailed out when everyone else started doing all the big adventures and put peer pressure on him to do the same. 'Couple of hundred bucks to do a bungee jump,' he exclaims in his Irish lilt. 'Thank God I didn't fall for that one.' He shakes his head at how close he came to being parted from his money on numerous occasions, and counts the days until his departure for Australia, where it is warmer. He goes out for dinner bundled in layers of clothes against the cold. Good thing he never tried tramping down in Fiordland.

While unpacking my bags I cannot help but notice the papers, which he has thrown in the bin between the two beds. I read the words 'Self-assessment Guide for Residence in New Zealand' and pull them out. He must have picked up the application forms for immigration to New Zealand in London on his way over. The Immigration Officer at New Zealand House has attached a note to the brown envelope informing him the current pass mark for immigration is twenty-six points. It sounds like the daily fluctuation of currency exchange rates, or the level of the stock market index. I sit on my bed and calculate points for a 'quick self-assessment' under the 'General Skills' category. I get the maximum twelve points for education and the maximum ten points for work experience. No one has offered me a job, so I lose those five potential additional points. Two points are offered for the capital I would bring over with me. No spouse, so I get no additional credits from a failed marriage and apparently zero credit for broken hearts either. If I married a Kiwi woman, I would not have to worry about calculating points at all; I would be in like Flynn. I barely squeak under the wire and only get two points for age; if I were fifteen years younger, I would get ten points. I add up the points and it comes to exactly twenty-six.

If I wanted to, I could settle here. But I'd have to make up my mind fast. If I wait another year, I'll be too old to get the paltry two points for just being warm and alive.

I pick up my poste-restante mail from the Christchurch central post office, the first letters I have had in five weeks. Included is a package with a home-made Advent calendar, which has messages written on some twenty-five sealed red envelopes to be opened and read each day until Christmas. I sort through this treasured mail while sitting on the steps of Cathedral Square. The letters drag me emotionally half a world away, and when I have finished reading them they leave me alone with my thoughts.

I listen vaguely as the Wizard, a bearded Christchurch character in an outrageous outfit, provocatively spouts off tired chauvinistic ideas about the place of women in society. Unlike Speakers Corner in London, no one heckles him. Perhaps they all agree. When the Wizard tires, another speaker replaces him. He climbs a stepladder he has brought with him and starts spouting how Jesus Christ came to earth to save us sinners. A young man in torn jeans and long hair ridicules him and the evangelist threatens the fellow with a thumping in return. The jeering continues until the evangelist steps down from the ladder and really does thump the persistent heckler. A shoving match ensues before the young man takes off, to mutter profanities under his breath from a safer distance. Satisfied, the proselytiser of goodwill towards all men climbs back on his stepladder.

He shakes his fist and points at the motley crew assembled in front of him. 'I'm sick of you people getting up my nose. And Jesus Christ' – his forefinger indicates the sky – 'is sick of people getting up his nose.' He dramatically thrusts with his forefinger as if he were trying to stick it up someone's nose. 'But I'm here to tell you in no uncertain terms, Jesus is going to get up your noses' – he points to us – 'like you wouldn't believe, on the Day of Reckoning.'

꙾

Recovered from whatever it is that ailed me, I hitchhike north up the eastern coast to Kaikoura. When the Kiwi nurse giving me a ride stops at a local gas station to fill the car with petrol, I pick up a copy of the *Northern Outlook*.

The front page is dominated by the headline: 'CAMPERS DIVE FOR COVER TO AVOID SHOTS FROM HELICOPTER'.

> Campers cowered behind a vehicle for protection against shots fired from a helicopter spotlighting a deer above the Loch Katrine bach settlement on Saturday night . . . At about 9.45 pm several shots were fired from a semi-automatic weapon in the helicopter as it followed the animal down the hill . . . A group of campers were gathered around a campfire on the beach. Some of these people took shelter behind a vehicle as the shooting got close. 'I've seen helicopters shooting deer in the area for thirty years, but this was the most blatant example of a flying cowboy I've ever seen,' a witness said.

I ask the nurse what a 'bach' is, pronouncing 'bach' as in Johann Sebastian Bach.

'Ah yeah, you mean a bach,' she replies, pronouncing it 'batch'. 'That's what you'd call a cabin or a cottage. They call it a crib in the woopwoops down south.'

I show her the article as we drink a couple of soft drinks. 'Dangerous out there,' I observe.

'Is it what!' she replies. 'Too many trigger-happy lunatics lurking around with loaded rifles, bad eyesight and even worse judgement. Got be an Armed Defender with a reflective red flak jacket and helmet to survive a bloody walk in the bush nowadays.'

I gather she isn't a hunter.

At the Kaikoura information office, the usual adventures are offered to tourists, but there is an innovative one I have not noticed before: 'Possum hunting'. For a few dollars you can get equipped with a gun, accompany a local psychotic and blast a few deadly possums out of the trees.

The settlement of Kaikoura is asleep. In the pre-dawn light I wander down to where fifteen other dolphin spotters have assembled to put on heavy wetsuits, flippers, goggles and masks. The wetsuits are still damp from yesterday's use. We are shivering and cold even before we board a vintage bus. As we drive to the boat, the sun flops lazily over the horizon, colouring the sea turquoise; the nearby snow-capped peaks of the Seaward Kaikoura Mountain range are cast in the warm light of dawn. It is an impressive setting even by New Zealand's high standards.

Our guide stands at the front of the bus, spouting her prepared speech: 'The visual splendour you see above water matches the opulence under the sea. Just off the coast is an ecological wonder, a marine-biologist's dream: easy access to whales, dolphins, seals, bird life and of course fish. All congregate in this area to feed off the phytoplankton, krill and other life forms rising with the deep ocean currents. Fifteen different species of marine mammals feast here, from giant sperm whales to tiny Hector's dolphins.'

Sitting silently in damp wetsuits, we wait for our boat to be launched. It is on a trailer, which is lowered by tractor down a ramp into Kaikoura's harbourless water. A fishing boat is in the process of being pulled out, a hapless man-sized shark draped over the bow. We all stare open-mouthed but no one says a thing.

Within twenty minutes of setting off into the South Pacific Ocean we reach a pod of dusky dolphins. They are easy to locate even from a distance; the ocean surface is roiling with their activity. Some are jumping high out of the water and landing on their backs with a splash, somersaulting forwards or backwards.

Our guide says: 'Although they are creatures of the wild, they are actually executing these acrobatics for the sheer fun of it. These are the awake dolphins, on the leading and lateral edges of the main pod. The main group of dolphins is calmly swimming, surfacing to exhale and inhale – in effect sleeping. There are probably four to five hundred dolphins in the pod at this time.'

We drift into their midst and the engines are switched off. The dolphins swim slowly by, the younger dolphins close to their mothers. The puffing of their collective breathing is the only sound. We could reach over the side of the boat and touch their backs. The boat circles in front of the pod again and this time we slip overboard as the dolphins come closer.

It seems unnatural jumping into the middle of the ocean like pre-packaged shark bait, with hundreds of wild dolphins swimming towards me. The cold water and the frenetic activity of the dolphins are startling. The first to make contact are the awake dolphins as their pale streamlined shapes torpedo past. We have been told that if we want them to stick around and play, we must do something unusual to arouse their curiosity: sing to them underwater, make squeaky sounds to communicate, dive beneath the surface, or swim around in circles after them.

Finally getting used to the cold and the ghostly shapes hurtling by, I dive underwater, not easy without weights to counteract the buoyant wetsuit. I submerge a couple of metres and half a dozen dolphins surround me. They move effortlessly and quickly, with the grace of underwater ballet dancers. One manoeuvres closer, curious, and stares long enough for me to make eye contact. It is so near I could hug it. There is an unmistakable sense of connection between us; two species with a higher level of intelligence. This experience is not like staring a cold-blooded fish in the eye.

Others advance, studying me as intensely as I examine them.

Their eyes reflect humour, accentuated by the upturned smile to their mouths. These warm-blooded animals have a presence about them; they seem almost cuddly, even if they are hairless and denizens of a totally different realm. Out of breath I surface, then plunge again, kicking my flippers in unison to imitate a dolphin's tail. The dolphins slip by with barely a propelling movement as I struggle to stay underwater in the wetsuit. At a depth of two metres, I twist upside down to see the surface of the ocean like a silvery waterbed mattress, with above me the dark shapes of swimming dolphins. They seem to beckon, inviting me to join them. Then, as if frustrated as much as I am by my ungainly physical limitations, they disappear into the depths with a flick of their tails.

I surface and remove my mask and snorkel. The other swimmers sing through their snorkels, as the guide told us, to keep the dolphins amused and hanging around. The high-pitched inflections are both muffled and strangely amplified by their snorkels. The ocean is alive with hundreds of dolphins playing, jumping and somersaulting around us. A six-foot blue shark swishes its tail languidly as it drifts through the pod.

Returning to shore, we sit shivering in our wetsuits with broad grins despite our frozen and purple noses. Back in warm, dry clothes again, I leisurely eat a colossal hokey-pokey ice cream with a couple of home-made chocolate biscuits, while perusing the local newspaper. An article on the front page catches my eye:

SHARK BITE ON DOLPHIN SWIM TRIP 'UNUSUAL'

An incident last Thursday, in which a German tourist was bitten by a shark while swimming with the dolphins, was reported to be highly unusual. A company spokesman said the man was swimming with the dolphins some four kilometres off the coast. He was swimming a little away from the main group when . . . a small blue shark bit him.

'The man felt something but didn't realise he had been bitten until he got into the boat and saw the blood,' the spokesman said. 'The doctor said it was a very clean cut, there was no flesh missing.' The man did not require hospitalisation and continued with his trip around the South Island after receiving medical attention and stitches to his right arm.

Good thing it was him. If I had been bitten by a shark, I would have noticed for sure.

⇒

From the guidebooks, Nelson would seem the ideal place to settle in New Zealand. It lives up to its reputation, being a quaint town with one of the highest amounts of sunny days in the country. For the first time since arriving in New Zealand, it's beginning to feel warm. I register at a popular backpackers lodge.

Around the swimming pool, half a dozen young lager louts in their early twenties, skinny bodies contrasting with budding swollen stomachs, recline languorously, partially anaesthetised by the contents of the empty beer cans lying in a mound at their feet. Medical researchers would be hard pressed to locate two synapsing neurones amongst the lot of them. They obviously don't care about the hole in the ozone layer, nor the burn factor, and their normally pale bodies are fried a nut-brown, tinged with radiation red.

My roommate, a pale Englishman in his early thirties, wears a polyester shirt buttoned to the neck, tight-fitting polyester slacks frayed at the pockets, black patent-leather shoes and a wide-brimmed perfectly white sun hat. He hugs a cheap plastic bag close to his hip, its strap wound securely over his head and shoulder. Other than the plastic bag, he seems to have few other possessions besides a pocket-sized computerised chess set.

Kiwi news is read on television. Behind the two newscasters is a map of the world from a New Zealander's perspective, with New Zealand at the centre of the world. Why not? But it is also magnified out of proportion so that it is – comfortingly – as big as Australia. At the end of the news, the weather forecast includes 'burn times': how long the average person needs to be exposed to the sun's rays before his, or her, skin begins to fry. Eleven minutes. You don't have to be exposed to nuclear radiation to die here. Mowing the lawn for fifteen minutes in the sunlight will get those free radicals going too, and with the ozone hole over the

Antarctic growing larger every year, those burn times are just a hint of what is coming.

My roommate is on his bed, knees drawn up to his chin, distractedly watching television while playing chess. He looks shrivelled, as if the television were sucking the life out of him. We talk without him taking his eyes off the telly. He tells me: 'I always travel light. Before checking in at the airline baggage counter, I fill my bags with plastic bottles full of water so I've got the maximum allowable luggage.' He smirks.

'Why?' I ask. Rather than being interesting, sharing a room with such strange people only intensifies my feeling of loneliness.

'Read the small print on your travel ticket,' he says. He turns to rummage in his plastic carrier bag, pulling out his airline ticket. 'The airline companies only compensate for lost luggage according to its weight. The heavier it is, the more you get back in compensation.'

I imagine him travelling the world, sitting in the aircraft cabin, fingers crossed that his bags stuffed with plastic bottles of water will get lost. He idly points the remote control at the television and channel surfs to a Maori-speaking programme. 'Why don't they speak English like they're supposed to,' he says, offended. I leave him huddled on his bed, channel surfing with a flick of his wrist.

ABEL TASMAN NATIONAL PARK

In the morning, psyched to start another track, I prepare a hot breakfast. I turn on the grill in the oven and place several slices of bread with cheddar cheese and tomato on the top rack, then quickly pack. My roommate is already immobilised in front of the television. Full of anticipation and also fully loaded, I wobble around the corner to pick up my mail from the Nelson post office. I prop my pack against a bench outside, sit in the sun and read my Christmas correspondence, which includes a gift from Norway, cards, some letters and a fax. It is strange to read how dark and miserable it is in Norway, Canada and London. How easy to forget, and a nice reminder of how lucky I am to be here. A Danish couple next to me open a package and pull out four candles for Advent, as well as home-made Christmas biscuits. When the girl sees these reminders of home, she starts to cry. Her boyfriend puts his arm around her shoulders to console her. A few minutes later, she is laughing and happy again as they read their correspondence together.

On the bus to the Abel Tasman National Park, I feel pangs of hunger and belatedly recall the toasted tomato and cheese sandwiches. In fact, I had not even taken them out of the oven. Being chronically impatient, as is my bad habit, I had even closed the oven door to get the cheese melting more quickly. What if the oven caught fire? What if the hostel went up in flames? Will the police be on the lookout for me? I slide back down into my seat and hide, just in case.

I distract myself from these twinges of guilt by glancing through the DOC brochure. Abel Janszoon Tasman, a Dutchman, was the first white man to 'discover' New Zealand in 1642. He saw no riches or trading opportunities in New Zealand and the Dutch authorities showed no further interest in developing the new territory. Imagine discovering a place like New Zealand and figuring it wasn't worth declaring ownership over. It was not until Captain Cook arrived, 125 years after Tasman, that any real exploration by the colonising European powers took place.

The path into Abel Tasman National Park is so well manicured that you could practically cruise the track on roller blades. Anchorage Hut is located in the bushes just off the end of a long curve of golden beach. Several kayaks are pulled up on the sand and more paddle in. The hut is almost full of kayakers and trampers. I find one of the few spaces left on the communal bunks, pull out my sleeping-bag and spread it on the mattress, claiming my spot for the night. Next to me a blonde, clad in a minute bikini, rummages through her pile of belongings. Her bikini is about as small as she could wear without redefining it as a G-string. I have a piece of disposable camera-lens tissue in my pocket which would be more effective as a bathing suit than both parts of her bikini combined. She has a perfect hourglass figure, the kind us guys are wont to fantasise about. She unfurls her sleeping-bag next to mine and then looks at me, her dark brown eyes contrasting with her long, curly blonde hair.

'Do you snore?' she asks. I deliberately keep my eyes on her nose, which in contrast to everything else about her is angular and freckled. 'Do you snore?' she repeats.

'No,' I gurgle. Why are men like this?

'Good,' she says. 'I don't like snorers.'

'Do you?' I enquire, my mind not wondering about her snoring at all.

'Snore?' she repeats.

'Yeah,' I manage to say, choking on the syllable. Men are so visual. I wonder if she can tell what I am thinking.

'No,' she replies.

'What's your name?' I ask, on an articulate roll.

'Candy,' she answers. I wonder what she is thinking. 'What's your name?' she asks.

'Candy,' I repeat, the logical side of my brain finally packing it in. 'I mean, Andrew.'

Nice recovery Andrew, but you're losing it fast and about to short-circuit big-time. Get a grip.

More trampers with backpacks arrive at the hut, but all the bunks are taken. Ten trampers are without an allocated mattress on the communal bunks and the DOC warden pulls out more stored mattresses and puts them on the porch. Several young boys staying in the adjacent campsite sway around the place with litre-sized soft-drink bottles on which they suck suspiciously frequently. One of them abruptly passes out in the bushes, having totally miscalculated his system's capacity for alcohol.

Candy sits outside on the porch steps, surrounded by four more drooling males: two Americans, a Canadian and a Dane. They are so busy flattering her that I involuntarily stand apart. This is the first track for all of them. She asks me which tracks I have done.

Given an opening, I answer as if naming nature products bought in a tramper's version of the Body Shop: 'Rakiura,

Milford, Caples, Routeburn, Kepler.' I don't tell them I tried to do the Banks Peninsula but got booted off. I am fast moving out of my role as 'new boy' and becoming somewhat of an authority, a veteran tramping guru.

'Which did you like best?' Candy asks.

I think about this and stroke my unkempt beard in a show of sagacity. 'It's like comparing apples and oranges. Depends on the weather, your mood, who else was in the huts. They're all different.' I am still not used to how these various tracks are neatly packaged, marketed and put on the shelves for consumption. 'Done the Milford' – as if that was all that was needed to explain the nature experience.

Candy asks me where else in the world I have travelled. When I tell her, she says: 'Sounds like you've got the travel bug.'

'It's not a bug. A bug is curable,' I reply.

They sit around a candle on the porch and show no signs of going to bed. An overweight German, with his daughter next to him, snores loudly and contentedly on one of the mattresses put out for the overflow of trampers. I withdraw from the conversation about the best places to stay in backpackers' Asia and walk the length of the beach and back. The peacefulness of the waves lapping on the empty shore, the sounds from the bush, the stars, all emphasise my solitude. It's an exquisite evening and it feels intense being alone on an idyllic beach under a black sky full of stars.

When I return the others are still talking. I brush my teeth then plug my ears with wax balls so that I cannot hear the snoring. Even inside the hut, it is cold. I slip into my heavy-duty sleeping-bag and am soon asleep. Sometime later I feel someone climb onto the bunk, then crawl into the flimsy sleeping-bag next to mine. I turn to see who has disturbed me and recognise Candy's curly blonde hair, strands of which are close enough to tickle my nose. I lift my head to see how crowded the mattresses are. On her side of the bunk is plenty of room, next to a couple who are huddled together, barely taking up any of their allotted mattress space. Ditto the couple next to me. There is plenty of elbow-room for Candy to sleep nice and secluded on her own designated mattress. I lie down again but she insinuates herself closer, her hands almost shoved under my body. I do not roll away. I think I hear her whimper, but I have wedged my earplugs firmly in place and cannot distinguish sounds effectively. I lie there absolutely still, too dopey to remove the earplugs and find out whether the murmuring is just the fantasy of a Lonely Guy who has been travelling on his own too long. For all I know, she could be whispering sweet nothings to me.

She is still asleep when I leave the hut.

Timing my departure perfectly to coincide with low tide, I cross the exposed mudflats rather than skirt the long way around the lagoon to the next hut. Halfway across, I become bogged in sloppy mud and have to slow down. I stub my toe on a hidden obstacle, lose my balance and slip. Trying to regain my equilibrium, my extended arms fluttering like a butterfly, I overextend myself and dive forwards, plastered to the mire by the weight of my top-heavy pack. I slowly get up on my hands and knees. My entire front, head to toe, is covered in slime and I silently extricate myself, scraping the mud from around my eyes, mouth, beard and out of my nostrils. I feel like Charlie Brown's mate, Pig-Pen.

When I reach the safety of hard ground on the other side of the lagoon, I watch gleefully as two trampers cross the expanse of mudflat, following my footsteps. Sure enough, about halfway across they too slow, lifting their legs in the gumbo like flies stuck on flypaper. Disappointingly, neither of them takes a nosedive.

I reach Awaroa Hut, to find another backpacker there. She takes one look as I come through the door, my entire front still covered in what looks and smells like dried cow shit, and ignores me. It's not easy to ignore someone in the limited space of an otherwise empty hut in the middle of the wilderness. But she manages it, somehow.

The trees are blackened in many areas in the forest, as if a fire had raged through the area, but they are clearly still alive. As I walk, a distinctive sweet smell lingers in the air. Inspecting the tree trunks closely, I can make out nodules from which hairs protrude, with tiny clear drops on the end. I dab a finger on several globules and then lick my finger, to taste a flavour like honey.

The eastern side of the park is too full, but this end is empty. Although I find this north-west part of the Abel Tasman Park more alluring than the other, more popular extremity, there is no one else to share the homestead-turned-DOC hut when I arrive that evening.

John, a retired local from Takaka now working as the hut warden during the summer months, checks my pass. His long hair curls over his square shoulders. He sits down with me, clearly interested in talking about the fauna and flora of the park: 'The small nodules you saw on the beech trees? They're formed by a female insect, who seals herself within the bark. She draws sap from the tree and excretes the excess through a fine hair-like thread, which you saw protruding from the trunk. The excrement you tasted forms in a little drop at the tip of the hair and is fed upon by birds and insects like bees and wasps. If the drop falls on the ground or the trunk of the tree or the surrounding vegetation, it nourishes the black sooty fungus. That's the black stuff.'

'And the sweet smell in those sections of the bush is the honey-dew?' I ask, as I boil water for tea.

'Yeah.'

I rummage in my pack and pull out a package of milk biscuits, hoping John will stay and talk for a while. I'm spending too much time on my own, and even if I have a lot of stuff to sort out in my life, there's only so much I can accomplish by being alone.

'Plenty of traps on the track,' I observe, while pouring two cups.

He takes a sip of tea before commenting. 'Ah yeah, some traps are for possums, some for stoats. I've got control over them now, but they were pretty bad. Possums practically sit up and beg from the trampers. Bit of a hard case, those possums. Even come into the hut to steal food out of packs.' He reaches into a breast pocket. 'Ciggie?'

'Don't smoke.' I hand him the opened package of biscuits. 'Where's the possum come from?' I ask. 'I thought there weren't any endemic mammals in New Zealand except bats.' I know the possums aren't endemic; I'm just making conversation.

John shakes his head and sips his tea, closing his eyes against the steam. 'Australian brushtail possum,' he answers. 'Ironically, they're protected in Australia but here, without natural enemies and lots of food, they've multiplied so successfully that there's some seventy million of them covering about 90 per cent of New Zealand.'

'That's the same number as the sheep you've got.'

'Exactly. That's why we have to get rid of them. Bloody useless. At least we can eat the sheep.'

I say, defending them: 'But they've got big eyes, and soft fur, like African bushbabies.'

'Marsupials,' John corrects. 'They have pouches and are nocturnal, feed at night.'

'That's why you see so many squashed on the road?'

'Get caught in the headlights of vehicles. Good thing too.' He dips a biscuit into his tea and chews on the soggy portion before finishing the rest.

'I've seen dead ones lying on the track.' I offer him another biscuit.

'Poisoned. Usually by 1080,' he says, as if this was a numeric combination of which everyone should know the meaning. 'Good bikkies,' he adds.

'1080?' I ask.

'Sodium monofluoroacetate. Supposed to be water-soluble.'

I nod, as if those big words explain it perfectly. Poison. I also try dipping my biscuit in my Sleepytime tea. It tastes funny. 'What's that do to the environment, other animals, birds?'

He shrugs, and suddenly sensitive to my question, says: 'What's the alternative? The possums are eating our forests away.'

'They look cute.' I'm not trying to provoke John, because they really do look cute, other than in DOC propaganda, which makes them look decidedly evil.

'They destroy our native plants and trees; snails, wetas and other invertebrates; bird eggs and chicks such as the kiwi, or those two oystercatchers you probably saw on the beach just now. Every time that dumb pair lay eggs the possums get 'em. Probably sit there watching and wait for them to lay their eggs. They also spread bovine tuberculosis, which threatens our dairy and meat industries.'

'So what can you do?'

'Shoot them, trap them, poison them. Whatever we do, it won't be enough. Bringing possums here has really stuffed up our nature.'

'Seems a bit harsh.'

His face flushes and I change the subject quickly. 'I thought I saw a marijuana plant beside the path today.'

'Ah yeah. You only saw one?' He laughs. 'There are fields of marijuana in the parks. You can make a thousand dollars from one marijuana plant. The marijuana growers keep one step ahead of the police and the possums. They began by protecting the gardens from possums by using razor-blade wire fencing. Then the possums found their way through that, so they started to use electric fencing. When the police flew their helicopters to search for marijuana fields, they located the gardens by listening to the electrical interference on their radios. So the growers got smart and used the electric fences only at night when the possums were out and the helicopters weren't. It's a cat and mouse game.' He is quiet for some time before he flicks his long hair off his shoulders and adds: 'Course, a lot of people think us DOC workers have got the best access to good growing areas.'

During the night there is a terrific rainstorm and before dawn the loud din of birdsong wakes me. It is impossible to sleep in on such a glorious day. I follow the track to the western end of the park. Steam rises from the damp forest floor as if there were vents under the fallen leaves. The slanting rays of the early-morning sun filter through the upper canopy of trees, illuminating the mist in a ghostly latticework of light and shadow. The rainforest reverberates with the assorted melodies of unseen birds. The sense of infinity in this ancient forest humbles me.

HEAPHY TRACK

There are so few cars in this corner of New Zealand that I almost have to walk instead of hitchhike all the way to Takaka, the hippie epicentre of the country. On the main street, a horse-drawn carriage passes by, constructed out of the rear axle of a car. Grey hair, a beard and bushy eyebrows disguise the driver's face, and he has a red kerchief wrapped around his neck. A long-haired grey dog sits on the seat next to him wearing an identical red scarf. They could be twins. The cart passes old Morris Minors, Hillmans, Anglias, Vauxhalls, Rovers, Humbers, Sunbeams, Land Rovers, Zephyrs, Oxfords, Austins, Triumphs and Bedfords. Half a dozen sheepdogs in the back of a ute bark noisily as the carthorse clip-clops by.

A minibus takes several of us trampers to the start of the Heaphy Track, a five-day walk which will lead us back to the West Coast. The track was a route used by the Maori; it is not just designed for tourists, there is some historic merit to it. En route, we stop by a spectacular gorge. As we climb out of the vehicle, our driver lectures us: 'Adventure tourism is the wrong kind of tourism for New Zealand. It's a fad. You can bungee jump anywhere in the world. Unspoiled nature is what we have that is unique. Look at this.' He points ahead of him. 'They've built this huge, ugly, steel contraption, just to bungee jump from. Why? It was such a picturesque place before, why not sit there and watch, meditate, or float down in a kayak or a canoe? People come all the way from Wellington now by helicopter to bungee jump from the thing, but the river's natural beauty is ruined.'

He's in the minority with his opinions in New Zealand as far as I can tell, although all of us murmur agreement.

It is addictive, this silent plodding in rainforests. There's an unmistakable feeling of contentment. Hours after I have started the track, it begins to pour with rain, just as I reach Perry Saddle Hut. Inside is a Kiwi family, a man named Wayne, his son and daughter, and also two Kiwi women, Myra and Linda. The latter, who are a delightful couple when they can be bothered to speak to us, spend most of the time unabashedly huddled together on a communal bunk. Their lustful indulgences are ineffectively disguised by sleeping-bags pulled carelessly over their bodies.

Wayne cooks up thick slabs of fresh beef each the size of an encyclopedia volume. Tired of packaged pasta and soup, I bought something different for this trip in one of the health stores in Takaka: dehydrated split peas with ham. I cook them the standard five minutes prescribed for any dried food but the meal is almost unpalatably salty, the peas hard like tiny pebbles. Hungry, I devour it anyway. Then, feeling incredibly thirsty, I drink a litre of water. I feel bloated, as if the vegetables are re-hydrating in my stomach. Wondering if I have done something wrong, I retrieve the plastic package from my litterbag. The split-pea and ham soup mix did include dehydrated ham, but the kilo of split peas requires soaking overnight, prior to cooking for some hours. I had soaked them no time at all and boiled them a scant five minutes, barely enough to put a dent in them. Now they are immersed in a litre of water like they are supposed to, except they are in my stomach. My intestines bubble as I sit and read the visitor's book, trying to ignore what I have done to myself.

My bloated abdomen becomes painfully distended. I toss and turn all night in agony as fermenting peas detonate, the implosions muffled by my trustworthy triple-layer sleeping-bag. Myra and Linda, my two bunkmates, are too absorbed in their nocturnal bawdiness to be bothered with my gastronomic problems. Occasionally an ankle, hand or fleshy protuberance appears from an angle I would least expect. I pull my sleeping-bag up to my nose, secretly observing their frantic ribaldry.

⤳

It rained, snowed and hailed during the night. Several times I was awakened by the howling of the wind, sure the roof would be ripped off the hut. Now it is calm again, snow dripping off the corrugated roof in wet lumps. My stomach is still sensitive and I attempt to keep my flatulence discreet, but as I roll my sleeping-bag from the bottom up, the lingering gas is expelled.

Catching up with Wayne and his family at Saxon Hut, I find him already cooking up an evening meal of sausages and chops, while his two kids play cards. Afterwards Wayne clears up; he seems to do everything. Although the 'kids' are at university, they are living at home and I gather the same routine exists there too: he does the work, they relax.

'Want to play caads?' the son asks.

'What?' I reply, busy scouring pots and pans with Wayne.

'Caads. You want to play caads?'

I shake my head. 'Say it one more time.'

Wayne interrupts. 'Cards. He wants to know if you want to play cards.' He repeats it in an accent I can understand.

'Oh, caards,' I reply. 'Sure.'

'Good as,' the son responds.

They teach me to play Last Card, and Assholes and Kings. Outside, a torrent of water inundates the forest. Technically, we are on the West Coast, where the rainfall is the heaviest in New Zealand. 'Pissing with rain,' the son says, looking out the window.

'Persisting,' his father corrects.

'What do you do for fun besides play cards?' I ask, sorting out my hand.

'Go hunting,' Polly the daughter replies, without batting an eye.

Myra and Linda arrive, dripping wet. Within minutes they are warmly huddled together on a bunk bed, their lusty embraces ignored as we try to resolve who is the Asshole and who is the King. There is nothing to remind us that it is almost Christmas. No radio, no television, no Christmas lights in the bush.

≥

Wayne has got into the habit of serving me a cup of tea in the mornings.

I walk the entire day on my own. It is definitely addictive, this walk into the depths of a rainforest. I feel my body must crave the oxygen, the ambience, something . . .

When I arrive at the next hut, the two kids are already playing cards and Wayne is busy frying up the remaining side of beef. I wouldn't be surprised if there was a whole steer in his pack. He asks: 'Did you see Linda and Myra?'

'They were still in bed when I left the hut this morning. I don't know how they do it.' I quickly add, so that he doesn't misunderstand me: 'I mean, leaving it so late yet getting from one hut to another so quickly.'

'Flat out like a lizard drinking,' Wayne replies, removing another chunk of beef from the iron frying pan. His kids wait expectantly with mouths open.

A couple of hours later Linda and Myra arrive. Immediately after unfurling their sleeping-bags, they go at it hammer and tongs.

≥

I do not feel alone in the rainforest. After looking about to see if anyone is watching, I try hugging a tree, my face pressed against the mossy solid trunk, arms wrapped around it. I do this for several minutes before letting go. It does not feel as strange as I thought it might: it feels good. Trees make good friends. I take another look around before trying it a second time – and see Linda and Myra standing hand in hand. Embarrassed, I smile at them. They theatrically shake their heads and happily continue tramping down the track on muscular legs I'd kill to exchange my own for.

The walk to Heaphy Hut includes a couple of crossings on swaying suspension bridges, skirting limestone cliffs and caves on one side, and the Heaphy River on the other. The rocks are so overgrown with vegetation that it is difficult to distinguish, in the subdued light of the dense rainforest, what is rock and what is plant matter. The roots of a huge tree drip over the limestone, like the dribblings of a melted wax candle over a wine bottle. I am not sure whether the cliffs are supporting the trees, or vice versa. The trees in turn are covered in parasitic plants, which extract nutrients from humus collected in the branches high above. Rocky clumps and vines, tentacles and roots, all are intermingled in a seething, silent mound of vegetation and rock. It does not take much imagination to see all kinds of terrifying creatures in their shapes and shadows.

Through a gap in the nikau palms, I catch sight of the wide Heaphy River opening out to the Tasman Sea. When I get to Heaphy Hut itself, I find it has a view over river and sea, protected from the offshore winds by the forest. Because the hut is shielded from the breeze, it is infested by sandflies so vicious I wouldn't be surprised if they could actually bark as well as bite. I walk along the river to the seashore, where huge breakers crash along endless kilometres of empty beach. Driftwood, probably from trees that have fallen into the river and been carried down to the sea, litters the beach, especially at the mouth of the river.

To avoid sleeping in the hut, I spend the best part of the afternoon building a windbreak on the spit of beach, where the river curls before it flows out to sea. Heaps of fantastically shaped driftwood provide ample construction material. The completed shelter is both useful against the burning rays of the sun and as a windbreak from the strong westerly wind.

An athletic Kiwi jogs across the sand, negotiating the tangle of driftwood to admire my handiwork. 'Choice,' he says. 'Cool. Wicked. Love it. Awesome, amazing, sweet as.' He is stoked, full on, rapt, to use the colloquial expressions. 'Cool' is a word he uses often, even when I introduce myself. I never thought there was anything inherently cool about my name.

'Rad shelter,' he says in conclusion.

'Crisp,' I say. I might as well coin a new exclamation, having given up on my ability to say 'cool' in a way that sounds remotely cool. I don't have the right emphasis on the 'kuh' part of the cool, I reckon.

'Crisp?' he repeats.

'Yeah, crisp. Means cool, but better than cool.'

'Crisp.' He repeats it several times, listening to its sound, the effect. 'Cool,' he concludes.

He jogs off through the wreckage of tree trunks, heading back to the hut. I set up my home for the night. The sun sets in a red ball over the Tasman Sea, just as an orange full moon rises over the river lagoon on the other side of the spit. I cook dinner in the middle of this celestial performance, then stretch out beside my shelter. I think about what my family and friends are doing over Christmas, as I lie on this remote beach on an empty coastline, so far, far away.

≥

The roar of waves collapsing on the beach awakens me. It's the day before Christmas. The sun shines and already it is warm. White-breasted shags nearby dry their wings in the sunlight. I slept exceptionally well, lying on a soft cushion of sand with a comfortable sea breeze keeping the insects away.

I shake the sandy grains from the sleeping-bag, roll it up, pack my backpack and walk to the hut. Most of the resident trampers, including Wayne and his kids, have already gone. Despite the pesky insects, Linda and Myra are still affectionately locked in a wrestler's embrace. I debate whether I should wait for them to disengage before I say goodbye, or just leave. I decide to continue down the track, knowing they will catch me up.

At the park entrance Wayne's wife waits for her husband and children. They offer me a ride to Karamea, the nearest settlement, where as a special Christmas treat I have already booked myself into something more up-market than a regular back-packers lodge. After passing up their invitation to continue with them to Westport, further south, I check in at the motel reception. With nothing better to do, I amble through the isolated village past a small wooden church and notice that Christmas Day service is at ten in the morning. There is not a lot to explore besides the church; Karamea is a straight road with a café and a grocery store. The woman who owns the café serves me a coffee, insists I try her cakes and will not let me pay for them. Two of her tousled-headed sons distract her: one rides his bike as fast as he can down the middle of the road, pulling the other on a skateboard, like a water skier on a rope behind a jet boat. The skateboarder careers recklessly between both sides of the deserted street; if he wipes out, he is going to cover himself with gravel rash.

'Git yer helmets on!' she yells at them. 'Going to do themselves an injury one day,' she says to me. 'Ever since they tar-sealed the road they think it's a slalom course.' The kids are barefoot and so is their mother. Everyone is. I feel conspicuously dressed up wearing sandals.

'Where're you staying?' she asks me.

'At the motel up the road.'

'What you doing tomorrow?'

I shrug self-consciously.

'Don't know what we're doing either, but if we get a barbie going, would you like to come?'

'That's kind of you.'

At any backpackers lodge I would have been with other home-less travellers and we would have made our own Christmas cheer. I walk back to the motel realising I have made a mistake booking into this more expensive accommodation. The few guests there seem unhappy and intent on forgetting Christmas. At least, I console myself, I do not have to cook. But sitting alone in the almost empty restaurant that night is a sad affair. In Norway, the Christmas Eve dinner would be the focus of Christmas. I try to forget that, but it reinforces the fact that I am alone in a desolate corner of this isolated country.

I escape to the lounge, where I watch television in the hope of catching something that might instil some seasonal cheer. But just as Christmas carols are about to be broadcast and my spirits are primed to perk up, the staff close down the main building of the motel. I am unceremoniously kicked out and the doors are locked.

I morosely close the door of my room, a prefabricated concrete cell without toilet, sink or television. It is a few minutes past midnight on Christmas Day. There are two minor consolations in this, I conclude as I undress, feeling sorry for myself. Firstly, it is twelve hours later in Europe and even later in Canada, so Christmas has not really begun back home. Secondly, it is the first occasion in two months that I have slept in my own room, in a real bed, with clean sheets. That must count for something.

It is hot and stuffy in the room and the windows, for some unknown reason, are cemented shut in their frames. Reluctant to sleep all night with the door ajar, I switch on the ceiling fan. Then I slip under the smooth, fresh-smelling sheets and lie restfully on my back. I turn off the bedside electric light, another luxury, and cradle my head on a feather pillow covered with white linen. The overhead fan picks up speed, wafting a comforting breeze over my body. I focus my mind on these small luxuries as the rhythmically circling blades rotate faster and faster.

Something flies off one of the fan blades and rudely flops over my face. I peel the rubbery, fishy-smelling thing off my nose, sit up and turn on the light. Hanging limply between my forefinger and thumb is a well-used, sticky condom.

CHRISTMAS DAY, KARAMEA

Credit on the hundred-dollar telephone card disappears within minutes; I call my father in Toronto, my mother in London and Kirsten in Norway. For several minutes I am Superman, flying from New Zealand to Canada, then England and Norway. Then there is silence, and I am back in my Clark Kent suit on a sunny day in a phone booth, a world away from the dark, snowy Christmas of those I love.

It has been snowy and cold since I arrived in New Zealand. Now it is hot and sunny and I am complaining. I am not sure I could get used to having Christmas in the summer season.

Perhaps home is not so much a place in space as a place in the heart, I muse as I head down the road to church, dressed in my backpacker's best. I enter the chapel and self-consciously slide into a back pew. The congregation, all couples or families, appraise the newcomer in their midst. An elderly woman in a colourful dress formally welcomes me and the warm reception chokes me up with memories of Christmas church services in Norway with my adopted Norwegian family. Those Scandinavian Yuletide images seem so confusingly idyllic now; the darkness countered by candlelight, the epitome of Christmas. Unlike Norway, where we would be bundled in overcoats and wool, the men here wear light polyester shirts, belted trousers tucked under ample bellies and worn, but polished, shoes. They must be farmers, judging by the backs of their necks, which are weathered and creased like elephant skin by the sun's searing rays. The women are resplendent in flowery cotton dresses. As if on cue a single bird sings vigorously outside the church.

A member of the congregation hesitantly begins to play a hymn on the organ. She finishes too soon, but we carry on, reading from the hymnbook before we stop, one by one. We wait for her to lead us again and she flips the music score back to the beginning. Her head nods up and down a couple of times as she mentally plays through the first few bars. We give it another try with better success, but halfway through she loses it, and we have to start from the beginning once more. By comparison, we sing 'Silent Night' almost flawlessly, although I have to reduce my voice to a whisper when I become emotional, remembering previous Christmases.

As I exit the church, nodding my head to acknowledge the

friendly greetings, a younger woman smiles and asks: 'Where are you from?'

'Canada.'

She introduces herself. 'Carrynne.'

'Where are you from?' I ask.

'Here. Karamea.' She introduces me to her husband, Evan: 'From Norway.' I greet him in Norwegian; he replies and we carry on conversing in Norwegian. 'If you're Canadian, why do you speak Norwegian?' Carrynne asks, surprised.

'Lived in Norway for five years.'

She asks: 'What are you doing today?'

'Nothing,' I reply, scratching my forehead. The other invitation was vague, just a possibility.

'You're welcome to spend the day with us. We're going back for Christmas lunch and there's more than enough food.'

'Are you sure?' I ask.

'Most definitely.'

That afternoon, Carrynne and her husband treat me like family at their cosy but magnificent wood-furnished house, which is on a hill overlooking a river. Two visiting Norwegian guests keep me happily chatting in Norwegian, making me feel slightly closer to 'home' in Norway. It is well into the evening before they drop me off at the motel.

When I return to my room there is a note pinned on the door. The café lady had come to collect me so as I could join her family for Christmas too.

BOXING DAY, WESTPORT

Eager to move out of the depressing motel, I catch a ride to Westport just down the coast from Karamea, and on the way back to Nelson. I find myself at the traditional Westport Boxing Day races. Here the Kiwis come in all shapes and sizes: weathered farmers whose portly bodies no longer fit too-tight, worn tweed jackets; their white-haired wives in print dresses, with wide-brimmed straw hats; bare-chested studs with tattooed biceps, shaved skulls and drug-dealer sunglasses. The latter guzzle jugs of beer in the back of flashy utes. Their women lie on their stomachs, legs displayed like barbequing Bratwurst sausages, with splotches of white skin on their lobster-red backs marking precisely where fingers covered in sunscreen have ranged. Other punters are more authentic, with shaggy beards, long hair, missing teeth and home-made tattoos.

The loudspeakers crackle, barely audible: 'Ladies and Gentlemen, there are only two minutes before the start of the next race, please make your investments.' Not bets but investments.

The scratchy recording of a trumpet heralds the start of another race. My 'investment' doubles.

Another announcement: 'A sum of cash has been found. If you have lost some money could you please come to the information booth to collect it.'

I check my pockets. Anywhere else in the world, that proclamation would be met with derision, especially at a racetrack. It is refreshing, this old-fashioned honesty on the West Coast of the South Island.

NELSON LAKES NATIONAL PARK

Outside Nelson, one could be forgiven for thinking one was in North America: whole hillsides have been clear-cut and replanted with Montana radiata pine. These trees grow faster in New Zealand than anywhere else; any vestige of native New Zealand on these hills has been lost through the widespread introduction of this imported pine species. Whole ecosystems are shrinking as whatever is left of native bush is chomped on by introduced species, particularly possums, deer and goats. Indigenous birds, reptiles, frogs and larger invertebrates fall victim to other introduced species like stoats, rats, cats and dogs.

New Zealand looks green and beautiful, but beneath the surface is an ecology that has been either destroyed or made insidiously vulnerable.

Arriving at St Arnaud in the late afternoon, I walk down to Kerr Bay and stand on the beach of Lake Rotoiti. Jet boats, skiers and motor boats zip backwards and forwards speedily in front of me. The scene, the sounds of engines and the drifting smell of petrol remind me vaguely of summers spent in cottage country in the lake district of Ontario, Canada.

Later in the evening, after dinner at my lodge, I head back down to the same beach. This time there are no boats on the lake and the overall effect is quite different. Instead of focusing on the water sports, I am more conscious of the wilderness, the snow-covered peaks on either side of the lake reflected in its still waters, the sounds of birds and the smell of fresh air. It is quiet and serene, in direct contrast to the activities earlier in the day. It reminds me now of Norway, where no motor boats are permitted on lakes, and especially not in national parks.

In the morning, I climb for hours. The views are spectacular, the temperature is perfect, the day being sunny but cool; yet I cannot escape the annoying buzz of the motor boats on the lake below. I am alone with no one else on the track, but the wilderness experience is diminished by the unrelenting hum of engines, just as that last day on the Milford Track had been. I feel old-fashioned and grouchy, but I cannot help imagining what it would be like if the only boats allowed on the lake were sailboats or canoes. I try to ignore the audible irritant but it bugs the hell out of me. It is only when I am over the crest of the mountain ridge and at aptly named Bushline Hut that a semblance of solitude pervades at last. I console myself with the fact that they have at least outlawed jet skis on the lake.

A solitary kea comes to pester me in the evening, strutting about looking for trouble. I rescue my boots and place them out of his reach inside the hut. He emits a plaintive cry before sulkily flapping away, presumably as pissed off with the day as I am.

≈

Leaving Bushline Hut, I enter a high alpine desert of brown rocks and patches of snow left behind from winter. The views from the top of the ridgeline are spectacular, with jewel-like coloured lakes at the bottom of steep scree slopes, resembling elegant turquoise necklaces. Ascending one last snowdrift to a saddle, I unexpectedly overlook Angelus Hut, which is set beside a semi-frozen, shimmering sapphire lake encompassed by a glacial cirque. I scramble down towards the lake, the semi-circle of snow-covered ridges reflecting and concentrating the sun so harshly that I can feel it burning into my skin.

Later, as I sit below a window in the shade of the hut, out of the searing sunlight, I overhear the conversation of two English couples inside. They had emigrated to South Africa a decade ago, and have now re-emigrated to New Zealand.

'Kiwis are unassuming compared to the English,' one of them comments.

'There's not the same stultifying sense of hierarchy here. If you make it, you make it and good on you,' another says.

One of the women adds: 'True, but I wanted to go back to South Africa when we first arrived in Auckland. The weather here still bothers me. It's so cold. Can't get used to doing all the housework either. Used to complain about the help in South Africa, but I'd be happy to have it now.'

A husband backs up the argument. 'Materially we were better off in South Africa, with good housing, swimming pools, fancy cars and tennis courts. The quality of life wasn't anything like we have here, though. We don't live in armed compounds any more, don't have walls, guns, dogs, guards or burglar bars. I used to worry every time she drove to the supermarket to buy groceries, in case she got carjacked. It's no life for children there, either. Here it's great, our children can go out and play and we don't

105

worry about them. You can't measure that freedom in material terms. Besides, we've got the same great outdoor life: rugby, cricket, barbies. Just don't have the problems.'

≶

Angelus has an auspicious ring to it and I decide to stay rather than move on. Just in case anything should happen to me, I leave a note in the hut, stating my intentions of climbing Mount Angelus. There is no marked path up to the summit. I follow bright yellow alpine buttercups growing along mountain streams, which empty into icy emerald lakes. Alpine daisies and New Zealand edelweiss flourish in the waterlogged areas.

It takes a couple of hours to reach the top of the mountain, which is 2075 metres high. Jagged peaks and lines of mountain ranges fade into the background and clouds hug the valley towards Nelson. The long curve of Golden Bay is visible in the distance, with snow-covered mountains looming in the foreground. Descending the same route, I slide down snowfields, using my hiking boots as impromptu skis. I happily shout and scream like a kid until I reach the rocky, boulder-strewn scree and the confines of the hut.

I search through my backpack for a suitable dinner. There are several packages of dried pasta, each with a misleading portrayal of a delectable meal on a plate: macaroni and cheese, fettuccine verdi, sour cream and chives, sour cream and mushrooms, cheese and black pepper, bacon carbonara, creamy mushrooms and bacon. Despite the fanciful names, each of these instant meals tastes and looks exactly the same. I should know; I've been eating them daily for the last two months. I take out the second of the split-pea and ham soups I bought in Takaka, the same meal that had given me severe abdominal problems on the Heaphy Track. This time I read the instructions carefully: 'Soak overnight or simmer for a minimum of two hours'. I haven't soaked it overnight, so I'll have to cook it for two hours. While the package of soup cost only a couple of dollars, the portable gas canisters cost eight. By the time I finish boiling these split peas until they are edible, this dinner will be the most expensive meal I have consumed on the trip.

Just as I get the water boiling, other trampers arrive. As they prepare their own dehydrated dinners, they can't help but notice that there is one portable gas stove burning for an inordinate length of time, unattended. Even after they have all finished cooking and eating, and even cleaned up after themselves, my solitary stove, lit long before their arrival, is still aflame.

I put the book down that I have been studiously reading and stir the gooey mush of peas.

'You've been cooking your soup for a couple of hours?' someone says, with the distinctive Kiwi inflection that renders a statement more of a question.

'I know.' I continue reading, as if cooking soup for hours on a portable gas canister is perfectly normal behaviour. 'Heaps of gas canisters in my pack. Trying to use them all up,' I say in explanation, without taking my eyes off the pages of my book. 'Lightens the load,' I add, trying not to appear any odder than I already am.

I decide to spend yet another lazy day and night at Angelus Hut. Everyone else packs and heads off in different directions, leaving me behind. It is the last day of the year, New Year's Eve. I climb the cirque's knife-sharp ridge, which encircles the half-frozen sapphire lake. Strands of mist rise vertically from the valley bottom, caught in invisible thermals. On the steepest and highest point on the rim, as I step on a large boulder, it gives way and lodges against the back of my calf, pinning me against the snow. Too frightened to move, I stand there carefully balancing the rock with my leg. Finally I manoeuvre out of its embrace, and once released it rolls, crashing down through the steep field of snow and ice. At first it careers like a sled, then cartwheels and bounces down, leaving a curious pattern in the snowfield, beginning like a snail's trail and ending up like a giant's leaping footprints. Curious, I time the descent. Thirty long seconds pass before the boulder crashes into the lake with a spectacular splash, the noise amplified by the sound chamber of the cirque. Ripples spreading out on the lake are absorbed by the remnants of soggy ice. Sometimes I scare myself when I realise how accident-prone I can be, although this was only a close call.

It is an anti-climax to return to the hut and find it still empty. Now that I'm getting to the point where I actually want to meet people, there aren't any around. It wouldn't be the first time I spent New Year's Eve in a cabin out in the wilderness; in fact, it's my preferred way of passing this particular night. But wonderful as it is here, in this setting, it would also be nice to share the evening with others; I mean, I feel a bit of a loser spending New Year's Eve all alone. I lie on a bunk bed and try unsuccessfully to read. Late in the afternoon, the first tramper arrives, entering the hut and dropping her pack heavily on the floor. She is covered in perspiration; her fair hair is wet around the temples and the back of her neck. She stands on a leg and stretches her quadriceps; despite the perspiration, she does not breathe hard and is clearly very fit. She's also pretty. I can't believe my luck, and introduce myself: 'Hi, I'm Andrew and I'm in this hut all by myself, with nowhere better to go on New Year's Eve.' I don't actually say anything other than my name, as she can probably figure the rest out for herself.

She tells me her name. 'Tania.'

I ask where she is from. She hesitates.

I have seen that equivocation before. 'Don't tell me, I know where you are from. Auckland,' I say, with the smugness of a magician pulling a rabbit out of a hat.

'How'd you know?' she asks, humouring me.

'Because any time a Kiwi hesitates to say where they come from, at least on the Mainland, then I know they come from Auckland.' People in rural New Zealand seem to view Aucklanders as if they come from a separate country.

'The Mainland?' She looks at me as if I am stupid, then balances on the other leg and stretches. 'Where's the Mainland?' she asks indulgently, as if dealing with someone mentally challenged.

'You know, the South Island,' I reply.

'Who told you the South Island's called the Mainland?' she asks, bending over and almost touching the wooden floorboards with her nose.

'All the Kiwis I meet.' I smile at her when she looks sideways at me from her upside-down perspective.

'And you've only been on the South Island, right?' She holds the position, blood rushing to her head.

'Right.'

'Figures.'

She unpacks, pulling her food and stove from the bottom of her pack. I ask her: 'It's New Year's Eve. Why aren't you with friends at a barbie?' As a Kiwi, she must have plenty of friends; it seems strange that she is here all by herself. If I were a cool Kiwi I'd invite her out for sure.

'The men stand around the barbie pretending to cook but all they really do is talk rugby or cricket. The women stand together in the kitchen and gossip. For a change, sometimes I go to a pub on New Year's Eve. It's such a pain in the arse, though. Guys won't take no for an answer. Last New Year's Eve I had to hit one over the head with a beer bottle.'

I take a step back to give her some more personal space. No point getting clobbered because of a cross-cultural misunderstanding.

'Sometimes you have to physically fight them off.'

I take another step backwards as a precautionary measure.

'I thought it was the Aussies who acted like that?'

'Ah yeah? You haven't seen a Kiwi in action, mate. You know what an Aussie bloke thinks is foreplay?'

'No.' I shrug my shoulders.

'Hey sheila, you awake?' She raises her eyebrows with contempt.

I laugh to demonstrate that I clearly know this is the most graceless form of foreplay.

She studies me. 'At least the Aussie asks if you're awake,' she adds, without a trace of irony.

NORTH ISLAND

JANUARY

≈

WELLINGTON

The ferry leaving Picton and the South Island slips through Marlborough Sounds, its bow slicing through splotches of krill red as bloodstains. Little blue penguins bob on their stomachs before diving out of harm's way. The ship's crewmen daintily dab paint at streaks of corrosion, talking to each other more than working. The deck of the ship throbs with the brute power of its engines and propellers.

I love ships, I love that feeling of going somewhere. My dad was a foreign correspondent. When we were kids we moved from one country and continent to another: Hong Kong to India, East Africa to London, Singapore to Canada. My father would put us and our mother aboard Norwegian cargo ships, with all our belongings, while he flew ahead to arrange accommodation and schooling. We children had the run of the cargo ships and the Norwegian crew spoiled us. The childhood memories remain: the red, white and blue Norwegian flag flapping at the stern while my brother and I fished in vain, or more successfully tied fishing lines to our flip-flops and let them surf in the ship's wake.

Nostalgically I am also reminded of the last time I was on a ferry, when I left Norway three months ago. I lean on the railings and feel the lurch in my emotions as I remember the scene. My eyes blur with the unexpected emotional charge. Just as I think I am getting better, a memory will suddenly resurface.

Then, just as now, the deck of the ship shuddered as the ferry gained momentum through the glassy water. I stood at the back of the boat and waved bravely until Kirsten became an indistinct image, and then only a memory. I watched as Nordmarka, the forested hills overlooking Oslo, receded into the distance. As we cruised down the fiord, the ship passed Sandvika and I caught a glimpse of the hundred-year-old wooden house we had rented. In the summer, we lived outside rather than inside, but in the dark winters the old wooden house had seemed a cosy haven, a refuge lit by candles and a fireplace. Our dog followed me everywhere and even when I worked at my desk in front of the window overlooking the fiord, alive with boats in the summer and skaters during the frozen winter, he would sit at my feet. I miss him. I miss her. Seeing our house again was my last contact with Kirsten. As the ship picked up speed, heading towards Denmark, I imagined her back there surrounded by the last remnants of our life together.

The ship continued down the coast, Nordmarka disappeared, and it was as if another tenuous connection had been cut, as if a page, another chapter, had been ripped out of my life. Except it was more than a page or a chapter. It felt as if the very book of my existence had fallen apart, the binding unglued, the pages loose, fluttering in the wind before settling in the churning wake of the ship and disappearing into the silent depths. My heart contracted and shrivelled, painfully buried in a body that seemed to me empty of life.

Kirsten had said I was like a sailor, always travelling, always about to leave as soon as I had arrived. Now I was gone for good.

To distract myself from these poignant memories, I focus my thoughts on this New Zealand ferry, crossing the Cook Strait between South and North Island. Also leaning against the rails is a young German and I engage him in conversation. We talk about our respective trips. After two months of exploring New Zealand, he doesn't want to return to Germany.

I ask him: 'What was the best and worst of New Zealand for you?'

He thinks for a long while. 'The worst, is how an unspoiled environment can be destroyed so much and so quickly.' He turns to look at me, as if to make sure that I am not offended. 'Of course, we did the same thing in Europe, and you did the same in North America, so perhaps we shouldn't criticise. But here it happened so recently, within only some generations, so it is more obvious.'

He has been so positive in describing his trip around New Zealand that I am surprised by his response, even though I had set him up with the negative question. 'And the best?'

He thinks even longer, before laughing. 'The best is that New Zealand is still so incredibly beautiful.' The ferry leans to port as it turns against the strong tide, negotiating a narrow passage through Marlborough Sounds. He continues, more positively: 'I would like to emigrate here. New Zealanders are lucky; there is so much space here, so few problems. It is the land of the future.'

I look forward to the North Island and meeting some of New Zealand's Maori. Apart from the Maori who returned my groceries in Te Anau, I have met none and seen few. Docking in Wellington is like entering another country. In contrast to the peacefulness of the little community of Picton, my introduction to the North Island is the hum of cars and the thumping of steel-belted tyres on a nearby flyover. Tall buildings cluster around the downtown core; residential suburbs are cantilevered out of the surrounding hills.

In the kitchen at the backpackers lodge, there is no excited chatter of international destinations or exchange of useful information. Everyone concentrates intently on cooking his or her own meals. The place has the depressing feel of a rooming house. A sign pinned to a door states: 'If you ask the obvious at reception you will pay a ten cent fine'. I finger a dollar in my pocket, tempted to demand a discount for a dozen quick dumb questions. The entourage of apparently unemployable poms lounging around the reception desk dissuades me, saving us all the hassle.

As the city winds down for the weekend, the bars fill with exhausted yuppies ready to blow off a week's steam. I do not want to head back to the depressing backpackers lodge, nor wander around Wellington on my own. It would be nice to meet some people, talk. Bracing myself, I walk into a smoke-filled bar with a deliberate if inexpert cool manner, but the smartly dressed men in pinstriped suits and women in skirts, lipstick and high heels are far too intimidating. No one says hello; I look out of place in my torn shorts, creased shirt and smelly sandals. In many places on the South Island I had worn the same grungy outfit and felt overdressed. Here, I feel not only underdressed but patently shabby.

I skulk out of the bar within minutes of walking in and timidly amble down city streets, trying to find something useful to do. The noise, traffic, buildings and general bustle are overwhelming; being out of the bush, I am suffering withdrawal symptoms. Buzzing sounds at traffic lights signal when to cross, and the intrusion of being ordered like a robot, when to walk and when to stop, seems far from the serene, meditative isolation of a walk in the forest. I am sure, though, I would adjust to all these assaults on the senses if I were back in the city for any length of time. It's amazing how adaptable human beings can be.

On Manners Mall, a pedestrian walkway, I sit on a bench outside a music shop, psychologically exhausted. With nothing better to do, I watch the parade of characters. Popular tunes, mostly sentimental love songs, drift out of the record store, pummelling my bruised heart again. Maori kids in homeboy-style jeans with the crotches drooping around the knees and sweatshirts with hoods pulled over their heads sit opposite me. They are bunched together beside a solitary tree, its trunk surrounded by concrete and enclosed by a wrought-iron cage.

NATIONAL PARK

I don't have the energy or the inclination to hitchhike out of the city, so I take the train instead. A smartly dressed father boards the train with his four kids. He looks like an accountant or a lawyer and the kids wear identical wraparound mirrored sunglasses.

The kids all say 'cool' as they enter the compartment. I sit and surreptitiously practise saying the word under my breath. Still can't get it right. The narrow-gauge train jolts forward and we wiggle our way out of Wellington.

The conductor sees me reading the newspaper. 'Mate, the only thing interesting you'll find in there is the cricket story,' he informs me.

Actually, I'm not reading at all. I'm thinking, and still practising how to say 'cool'. 'Which cricket game was that?' I ask, jolted out of my solipsistic world and trying not to appear eternally thankful that someone is talking to me, making my solitary plight less obvious.

He looks at me incredulously. 'Between Pakistan and Australia.' He then proceeds to tell me all about it. He is capable of recounting every over, every bowler, every batsman, every shot, where it went, and who caught it, going into such excruciating detail that, when he finishes, I do not even know who actually won the game.

I get up and twitch down the aisle of the jostling train like an erratic ball in a pinball machine. There is an observation deck at the back, which looks as if the rear section of the carriage has been removed, with just a plate-glass window remaining. It is a bit like gazing out of the end of a long goldfish tank. A sofa shaped like a horseshoe allows passengers to sit and view the scenery. Here the father and his wraparound-sunglasses family have ensconced themselves, with playing cards, cans of soft drink and potato-chip packets strewn across the central table. Two of the four kids squabble. I squeeze in beside the father. He asks: 'Where you from?'

'Canada,' I answer.

'Kuh-ool,' the daughter observes. She is only ten or eleven, but she's sussed me out, I can tell by the look of disdain on her face.

'Where are you from?' I ask in return.

'Auckland,' she replies, and without giving me a chance to say kuh-ool back, she asks, 'Where are you from in Canada?'

'Ottawa,' I say. But that was ten years ago; I'm leaving out the last few years from the biography. I'm not going to explain the intimate details of why I emigrated to Norway and then fled to this bratty little smart-ass.

'Where's that?' the daughter asks her father, peering at him through her sunglasses.

'It's the capital, like Wellington.'

'Know why Wellington is the capital of New Zealand?' the daughter asks, turning to me. My twinned reflections peer back from the two mirrored convex sunglass lenses, my double bulbous noses protruding out of proportion to my distorted faces.

'No,' I reply, waiting for her punch line.

'Because Auckland lets it,' she says smiling.

'Crisp,' I reply.

'Crisp?'

'Yeah, crisp. It means cool, except if you're really cool, you say crisp instead of cool,' I tell her, to keep her off-balance. She too can spread the gospel according to Saint Andrew.

Her father looks over as if to warn her that I'm pulling her leg, but she has taken the bait, hook, line and sinker. 'Crisp,' she enunciates, trying the word out for size and liking the sound of it. 'Crisp,' she repeats, clearly dying to try it out on her friends. Coining a new word for cool gives me a cachet, contradicting her assessment of me as being totally uncool.

The conductor interrupts over the speaker: '. . . Bridge is 281 metres in length and 79 metres high.' We stare out the glass of the back window as the train clatters over the yawning chasm beneath. One of these bridges collapsed some years ago. I cross my fingers and trust the wooden trestles supporting us hold out.

The girl sees me. 'Why are you crossing your fingers?' she asks.

Why are kids so observant?

'I just hope the guys who built the wooden bridge used the right glue,' I reply.

The train stops at a station called National Park, an isolated community which will be my base for the next couple of weeks. The platform is full of four-wheel ATVs and trail bikes. It is odd, in my view, to arrive at a railway station called National Park and discover wilderness-intrusive vehicles. Hand-painted signs advertise how much it costs to hire them. Another large sign says:

> Attention railway passengers. This railway station, bikes, animals, and property are all PRIVATELY OWNED. This is a four-wheeler and trail-bike business, and we live here. This is a private home and not a railway station. Please refrain from smoking and dropping your butts and we will refrain from dropping our butts on your porch.

I am the only person to disembark and the conductor, who doubles as a baggage handler, shoves my backpack to the door of the baggage wagon.

'Strewth,' he says. 'What have you got in there, your grandmother?'

'Uh-uh. My computer.' I grab the pack. 'Do you mind helping me hoist this on my back?'

I must have several kilos worth of maps, books, magazines and brochures stuffed into the bottom of the plastic lining bag. By the time I finish this trip, with the ballast the pack is gaining and the weight I am losing, I will weigh considerably less than the pack will. The conductor manoeuvres the pack to the edge of the carriage, holding it upright while I slip my arms into the shoulder straps. I take the weight and stagger reluctantly off, barely able to remain upright.

Despite the ponderous clouds above, the evening sky to the west is clear, lighting up the volcanic slopes with its sharp evening light. While the South Island's mountains were pushed up gradually by shifting plates in the earth's crust, those in the North Island were formed by violent and dramatic volcanic explosions caused by earthquakes and subterranean upheavals along a huge, central plateau.

I totter to the nearest backpackers lodge. Walking into the

lounge, I recognise someone – the Englishman walking the length of New Zealand. He is deeply tanned and sits by himself on a sofa. He does not talk to anyone; I say hello but he barely responds. I wonder if he is catatonic because of this walk, or if he is equally reticent at home.

That evening I climb into an upper bunk bed. My Italian bunk-mate below sleeps fitfully, and with every toss and turn of his considerable mass, he shakes the rickety bunk. Each time I panic, believing it is an earthquake; given my reading about the geology of the region, the misapprehension is forgivable. I ease myself to sleep by rationalising that if there were an earthquake and the bunk collapsed, at least I would have a soft landing.

TONGARIRO NORTHERN CIRCUIT

Tongariro National Park is comprised of three volcanoes, including Mount Ruapehu, the highest mountain in the North Island. All three volcanoes have erupted recently. Lava flowed from Mount Ngauruhoe in the Christmas Eve eruption, which destroyed the Tangiwai Train Bridge in 1954. That was followed more recently by large ash eruptions in 1974 and 1975.

The sky is blue and the volcano summits unclouded. I climb into the backpackers shuttle bus and we drive to the parking lot just before Mangatepopo Hut. Here hundreds of trampers set off, most of them walking the Tongariro Crossing, enticed by DOC marketing. While the Milford Track is advertised as the finest walk in the world, the Tongariro Crossing is billed as the finest one-day walk in New Zealand.

There is a never-ending line of trampers on the track, easily visible in their multi-coloured jackets. From the saddle, before it descends to Blue Lake, I divert to scramble up the slopes of Ngauruhoe. Loose cinders, black, red and brown, give way under my feet; with each step up I seem to slide half a step back. Looking up at the summit of this perfect, cone-shaped volcano, I see what could be mistaken for mist on a normal day, but with this clear cobalt-blue sky, it can only be a fumarole. It is like a child's concept of a volcano, a rounded-off pyramid with 'smoke' coming out of the apex.

From the summit of Ngauruhoe, I see to the north a moonscape of reddish-brown craters, deserts and snowfields, interspersed with brilliant emerald and turquoise crater lakes. To the southeast is the desolate Rangipo Desert, its shifting black sands flanked by the ten thousand-year-old Upper and Lower Tama lakes. Past the large, deep-blue lakes are the snow-covered, glacial slopes of Mount Ruapehu, which last erupted only some months ago. Far to the west, 155 kilometres away, I can clearly see the volcano Mount Taranaki, also known as Mount Egmont. While taking in this vista, I absent-mindedly step towards the steaming vent, into a natural volcanic sauna. The hidden force which shaped this cone of earth still lurks dormant, waiting to explode. Ngauruhoe is said to erupt every nine years, sending columns of ash several kilometres in the air. There should have been an eruption in 1984, and another in 1993, but neither occurred, so we are overdue for one now. Astride the leaking anus of this potentially active volcano, it occurs to me in mid-split that just the slightest puff of flatulence from Mount Ngauruhoe, at this particular point in time, would blow me away with little to show as evidence.

I jump off the volcano's privates and scramble down the crumbling slopes. Still full of energy, I climb both windswept peaks of Tongariro and finally descend to Ketetahi Hut late in the afternoon.

Meri, a young Maori DOC warden, checks my hut pass.

'You're the first Maori I've really had the chance to talk to,' I tell her. All official Government signs and documents are in both English and Maori, but in the South Island it seemed a made-up language; I never heard anyone use it. 'Can you speak Maori?' I ask.

'Of course.' She says a couple of sentences in Maori and then laughs. 'Did you understand?'

I shake my head.

'I said' – she gestures with both hands – 'that's where I live.' One arm is outstretched, indicating with a forefinger; the other arm points in the same direction, but is bent at the elbow, fingers by her head, almost in the stance of someone pulling the string of a bow. She sights her imaginary arrow at a red roof in the valley below. 'That's my dad's place.'

I look down and then over at the Ketetahi Hot Springs. A DOC sign at the hut had spelt out a prohibition regarding the springs, but without an explanation. 'Why is it forbidden to walk to the ridge overlooking the springs?' I ask.

'It's not up to me to say. The elders of the Ngati Tuwharetoa Trust have to decide.'

'Ngati Tuwharetoa?'

'The local tribe.' She moves all the time, unable to stand still, communicating as much with her hands, eyes, eyebrows and body as in speech.

'But what's it all about?'

'The springs are on private land, which belongs to the Ngati Tuwharetoa.' When she says 'private land' it has the force of 'PRIVATE LAND!', as if she had just yelled it rather than said it. I imagine it is an oft-repeated phrase. I accept her explanation, although to be within twenty metres of the springs, to see the steam rising and to hear the fumaroles hissing and boiling, then not be permitted to walk up and look, seems an obvious provocation to trampers. 'It's up to DOC to work it out with the elders of the tribe,' she adds. She is clearly uncomfortable with the topic.

However, when all the day trippers have gone, Meri relents and offers to take me to the springs. We walk down the path to an official green-and-yellow DOC sign, which reads 'The area beyond this sign known as Ketetahi Hot Springs is private land. Permission has been given by the Ketetahi Trustees for trampers to walk the next 400 metres of track, which passes through their land.'

The sign has been defaced: 'private' has been crossed out, and 'our' has been scratched into the green paint. The word 'their' has also been obliterated, and 'God's' added.

'The hot springs are created by rainwater seeping through cracks in the earth, heated by hot magma to form steam, which escapes out of the unseen underground holes,' Meri explains loudly, over the hissing steam.

She stares distractedly at the path below us. A small stone wall has been built across it, more as a symbol than a real barrier. 'I think I saw some trampers coming up the path. I don't see them any more. They must be in the pools.' Her lips are drawn tight and her eyes glint angrily. 'I better go and check.'

She takes off and returns minutes later, out of breath and perspiring. Several people descend the path out of the park.

'They were there sure enough,' she says.

'What'd you do?'

'Stood on the ridge and told them to get out. They pretended they couldn't hear me but they got the message in the end.'

'What'd you tell them?'

'Get out of the hot springs, you are on PRIVATE LAND!'

'I guess you have to chase people out every day.'

'Yeah. It's the worst part of the job. Usually I just lock myself in my cabin and ignore everyone. It's too much aggro arguing with them.'

We continue up to the hut, where Meri explains Maori culture and customs as I sit outside with a Swiss woman and a German couple. She imparts so much information it is impossible to absorb it all. When I start taking notes, it encourages her to talk more.

'Long before the Maori came here, the gods had the possession of the land.' She stands up as she talks, as if too restless to sit. She points with a sweeping motion of her hand to the landscape bathed in the late-afternoon light. 'Several of these mighty gods, including these volcanoes' – she theatrically indicates the mountains above us – 'stood in a group for centuries, until one day Taranaki attempted to carry off Phanga, the wife of Tongariro. Up to this time, the mountains had lived together with their families in friendship. But this treacherous behaviour caused conflict, and in the battle that followed, Taranaki went down to Wanganui on the coast, drawing a furrow behind him, through which the Whanganui River flows.' She moves in a visual display of the god's actions. 'He then fled along the coast until he found rest and peace. In solitary loneliness he now stands under the name of Mount Taranaki.' Meri says all this with reverence, as if it were gospel.

'What's it like going down the Whanganui River?' I ask.

She shakes her head. 'Never been down it. Wouldn't dare, too many spirits there for me. But you should try it.'

'Why should I try it?'

'If you want to see Maori customs, you should canoe down the Whanganui River. You'll see what I'm talking about, a real Maori village.' She says it with finality.

The sun sets and the sky is emptied of light. In the distance, we see the lights of the town of Taupo sparkling across the other side of Lake Taupo.

Before we go inside for the night, Meri says: 'That was a primo evening.'

'Despite the hassles.'

'Yeah, despite the hassles. It was primo talking to you,' she repeats, eyes flashing in the dark. 'It's the first night working here that I've stayed up so late.' She is still standing and we have been talking for hours.

'It was radical talking to you, too,' I reply, picking up her vocabulary.

She turns around, looks at the stars and says: 'Yeah. Choice.'

'Crisp,' I add.

I have to retrace part of my route to continue the Tongariro Northern Circuit to the Emerald Lakes, where I divert down towards Oturere Hut. A wind blows ferociously, threatening to knock me off my feet. Unlike yesterday, impenetrable clouds are so thick they seem to congeal over the mountains, adding a mysterious mood to this barren, desolate landscape. The mist disguises a wilderness of lava rocks, a bleak moonscape of gravel fields with a dry sand river giving off steam. The sand is hot from the steam, I discover when I kneel down and dig my hand into the riverbed. As I do this I hear a strange cry, almost an electronic sound, and guess it must be a magpie, although it is hidden from view.

I arrive at the spot where tourism began in the Tongariro National Park in 1901, with the building of the original Waihohonu Hut. Early tourists, doing the 'Grand Tour', took paddle steamers from the south-west coast of the North Island, up the Whanganui River to Pipiriki, and from there by coach and horseback to Waihohonu Hut. The completion of the main trunk railway in 1908 changed the focus of the volcanic park from the eastern slopes to the west, with National Park as the railway's stopoff point. Now that railway station has been privatised and trail bikes and ATVs are rented from the former whistle-stop.

The sky clears in the evening; the volcanic summit of Mount Ruapehu, with its steaming, vaporous edges, is gilded gold and backlit by the setting sun. The noise of the rushing river drowns all other sounds.

Sunrise lights up Ruapehu in a cold blue sky. Water left in the outdoor sink of Waihohonu Hut has frozen overnight. Leaving, I come across a warning sign:

> Volcanic activity. Lahar (mud and debris) flow paths exist in valleys on this track. If threatened, move to higher ground. Toxic gas can cause respiratory problems around and downwind from the crater. Ash layers can create unstable snow conditions.

In September 1995 Ruapehu blew, fifty years after its last eruption. Thousands of terrified skiers watched as lahars poured down three different routes. Steam, silt from the crater lake in the middle of the volcano, rocks and ash were thrown into the sky and the lake broke its containing walls. Skiing was abandoned, with volcanic activity continuing over the next month. Then Ruapehu entered a quiet phase until June 1996, when it again blew its top, resulting in massive ash explosions and fire fountains. Volcanic ash covered the snowfields, closing down the two commercial ski fields. Just a friendly little reminder that New Zealand is sitting on a powder keg.

～

The imposing edifice of the Grand Chateau Hotel dominates the village of Whakapapa (pronounced something like Fuck-a-papa, which makes it one of the few Maori place names that is easy to remember). The hotel appears empty and no one stops me from wandering around its cavernous interior, which boasts a massive lounge with plush carpeting, chandeliers and floor-to-ceiling windows. Outside are manicured lawns and a golf course. Opened in 1929, the hotel, which was modelled on those in Banff and Lake Louise in Canada, offered ostentation never before seen in the country. Through the windowed door separating the lounge from the dining hall, I see a few Japanese eating sushi in the restaurant. They stare at me, with my boots and legs muddy, loaded with my heavy backpack and sporting my usual unwashed, lopsided tramper-head. I stare back at them.

At the information centre in Whakapapa, I listen as a guide reads from a leaflet on the history of the national park.

'The volcanic mountains, Tongariro, Ngauruhoe and Ruapehu, came to personify the ancestors of the Maori people and were held in the deepest respect and awe. Few journeys were made into the mountains other than to collect *titi* (mutton-bird) from Tama Lakes and to bathe in the Ketetahi Hot Springs. So sacred were the mountains that the Maori would not even look at them when passing through Rangipo Desert. They shielded their vision with leaves, did not eat, and did not use the wood they found. Many Europeans had little sympathy for the awe in which the Maori held their sacred mountains. In 1839, John Bidwell became the first European to climb one of the volcanoes, Ngauruhoe.

'Horonuku Te Heuheu, the local chief, was outraged at the infringement of his ancestral *mana*. He had established ownership of these sacred mountains from other tribes and saw the pakeha development coming closer. As paramount chief of the Ngati Tuwharetoa, the tribe of the area surrounding the Tongariro mountains, Te Heuheu discussed the problem with his son-in-law, Lawrence Grace, who was an MP for Tauranga at the time. Grace agreed that it was undesirable to permit the mountains to be dealt with in the ordinary way. They should be regarded as *tapu* from private hands. He said to Te Heuheu:

' "Why not make them a *tapu* place of the Crown? A sacred place under the *mana* of the Queen. The only possible way to preserve them forever is to give them to the government as a reserve and park, to be the property of all the people of New Zealand, in memory of Te Heuheu and his Tribe."

'And so, on 23 September 1887, Te Heuheu formally offered the mountains to the crown as a national park, the first of its kind in New Zealand.'

When Peter, the owner of the backpackers lodge, comes to pick me up in his shuttle bus, I enquire about the Ketetahi Hot Springs issue. He replies as he drives his shuttle van out of Whakapapa village: 'Ah yeah, that's nothing more than a question of greed. It's ridiculous. Now we are giving everything back to the Maori, even paying them royalties for fishing miles offshore at depths that you can't tell me the Maori were fishing two hundred years ago.' He shakes his head angrily. 'I reckon that's why there's so much talk of New Zealand becoming a republic, so we don't have to adhere to the Waitangi Treaty.' We drive along an empty road adorned with tall toitoi grasses.

'You mean it's the British courts deciding these issues?'

Peter's jaw is set. 'The Waitangi Treaty was signed by the British and the Maori in 1840. It's got nothing to do with us pakeha now, but we have to sit back while all these negotiations go on and on, trying to decide who owns what.'

'What negotiations?' I ignore the scenery, more fascinated by the conversation.

'The Waitangi Tribunal. They're supposed to sort it all out but they're giving everything back to the Maori. If we don't give it back, it'll go to the Maori's court of last resort, the Privy Council in England, because it's a British court and the Waitangi Treaty was a British treaty. The British want to look good, it's no skin off their nose handing back all this land.'

'But if New Zealanders didn't have the well-established British laws and the Privy Council as a court of final arbitration, maybe foreign investors wouldn't have so much confidence investing in the new Republic of New Zealand either.' For the first time in New Zealand, I feel as if I am starting to get under the skin of white Kiwis. The friendly banter fades when the land issue comes up.

'The Maori just want money,' he repeats.

'But you're making money off the volcanoes. Trampers doing the Tongariro Crossing don't pay anything to DOC, but we pay you to overnight before and after the track, to drive us to the start of the track and to pick us up.'

'I have to pay DOC for each person I drop off.'

'You do?' I ask.

'Yeah.'

'How much?'

'Fifty cents.'

'That's not much.'

'It's something,' he replies.

'When do you pay them?'

'It's on the honour system. We keep track of how many trampers we bring in.' He stops at a crossroads, despite there being no traffic in sight, before turning towards National Park. I believe Peter would be meticulously honest about paying, but it seems a ridiculously small sum.

As if giving vent to his anger, he makes no attempt to avoid a possum carcass on the road. 'Just making sure it's dead,' he says, as we drive over the body, flattening it with a double thump of tyres. He looks in the rear-view mirror and adds: 'The only natural enemy of the possum in New Zealand. The steel-belted radial.'

To his credit, Peter goes out of his way to show me the site of a Maori *pa*, a balustrade built to fight off the British. The old Maori stronghold is overgrown with grass now, but the walls, the ramparts of the small fortification, are still plainly visible. A modest sign informs visitors that buried in the grounds are the bodies of Maori warriors who died fighting for their land. There are no formal monuments, no gravestones, no names, no dates. It seems inconsistent, with all the impressive monuments to the New Zealanders who died so bravely in the First and Second World Wars, that there is nothing more here than this simple symbol to the nameless Maori, who died equally bravely fighting for their land.

In the evening, I walk around the sleepy community of National Park. Down the road in an empty paddock an old truck has been converted to a house, complete with chimney and wooden shingles on the peaked top half, just like a proper roof. The sides of the truck have been pulled out, like shelves in a cupboard, expanding the size of the interior to almost three times the truck's width. The surrounding paddock is overgrown, but the mobile home looks better tended than the adjacent shanty-like dwellings, the gardens of which are decorated with rusty engine blocks and mud-splattered ATVs. Bored-looking dogs tied up in the yards bark at me as I walk by.

Cars and utes are parked outside the National Cosmopolitan Club. Curious, I peek inside a smoke-filled room to see a dozen bulky men crowded around a table with several jugs of beer. The men have bloated beer stomachs hanging over tight stubbies, massive thighs and oversized biceps decorated with tattoos. All of them seem to have missing teeth and shaggy hair. There are equal numbers of Maori and whites, although it is not easy to distinguish one from the other. The interior walls of the clubhouse are adorned with magnificent heads of red deer stags and wild pigs.

A Maori beckons me in. 'Want a beer?'

It's too late to beat a hasty retreat. 'Sure.'

I follow him and take a place at the bar. He returns behind the counter and reaches over to shake my hand. 'Welcome to the Cosi Club.' He pours me a beer. 'So, what are you doing round here?'

'Travelling around New Zealand for four months.'

'Ah yeah? Where you been?'

'All over the South Island. Now I'm slowly making my way up through the North Island.' Then I ask: 'What's the story with the Ketetahi Hot Springs?'

He looks around him to make sure he is out of earshot of anyone else. He is big and handsome, with the square jaw, smallish nose and olive skin typical of a Maori. 'Ah yeah, that's easy enough. The iwi, that's our local tribe, and the trustees of the Ngati Tuwharetoa want DOC to come to the party.'

'Come to the party?'

He continues quietly, turning away from the rough characters at the bar ordering drinks. 'The iwi are fed up with DOC, outfitters, lodges and air-charter companies sucking as much money as they can from the Tongariro National Park. It was deeded over as a gift, not to make money out of it. Everyone charges for everything, but the local iwi get nothing.'

He falls silent when one of the customers approaches the bar, serves him, then continues: 'The elders mostly want to close the springs and make it *tapu*, sacred, like it was in the old days. A spiritual retreat for the Ngati Tuwharetoa.' He shrugs. 'But the younger members of the tribe don't want to listen to them. At meetings, the young ones are often rude, shouting down the elders. Many, not all, of the younger ones want to turn the springs into a moneymaking venture based on the spring's healing properties. They see DOC, the lodge owners and outfitters all making money off the volcano, so they reckon they could turn it into a spa, like in Rotorua, and earn big money. The tribe can't agree on what to do, so they've let it drop for over a year now.'

'That's a long time.'

'Not for us.' He steps back from the bar defiantly. 'Our people are patient.'

Peter at the backpackers lodge had told me that the outfitters, tour operators and lodge owners were impatient for a decision one way or another, so they could plan what to offer tourists and market it. For them, the impasse was the least desirable outcome, worse than being told they could no longer use the springs.

I repeat what Peter had told me: 'Many pakeha are upset about the Waitangi Tribunal's decisions in favour of the Maori. For example on fishing stocks that are caught miles out at sea, and at depths where Maori never could have fished traditionally before. They say this reflects the absurd lengths the tribunal is taking to make amends and that it's not fair.'

The bartender smiles as he leans towards me, fixing his eyes on mine. 'That's OK, let the pakeha fight for it back in court. Now they know how it feels.' He laughs but his eyes flash anger.

RUAPEHU

Black clouds hang low to the ground, hiding the mountains from view. I catch a ride to Whakapapa village up the Bruce Road, which ascends to the Upper Bruce parking lot. The ski-resort's upper chairlifts are hidden in clouds, the grey and black summer landscape a lunar jumble of volcanic rock boulders, sharp pinnacles, deep cracks, bottomless gullies and cliffs. There is nothing green, growing or alive. The ski-lifts are a bizarre sight, their steel pilings sprouting from volcanic boulders the size of houses. Admittedly it is summer now, and during the winter this confusion of broken rocks would be covered in snow, but it is difficult to imagine anyone skiing here. Ski chalets, accessory shops and rental facilities have mushroomed amidst the mass of tumbled boulders. I walk up to the mist-shrouded chairlift, take a seat and am whisked effortlessly into the fog. There is nothing visible as I ascend until I break above the clouds into a clear blue sky.

Nearby, Ngauruhoe is a perfectly shaped cone, protruding out of the solid mattress of cloud. I jump off the first chairlift and climb onto another, which carries me over a tumble of massive rocks that have been dynamited to form a ski run. I ascend so easily and quickly to 2000 metres that I must equalise my eardrums. From the top, a T-bar lift operates in the winter, shuttling skiers another 700 metres to the summit. I am only a short distance below the top of the volcano and tread through fresh and increasingly deep snow up to the Notch, which overlooks the huge crater and the Whakapapa, Mangatoetoenui and Whangahu glaciers. From Glacier Knob, I look back towards Tongariro and Ngauruhoe, and regret not climbing up from the bottom of this volcano as well. Within a short time, I have climbed the ridge separating Whakapapa Glacier and the Summit Plateau, a carved-out cirque which itself resembles the centre of a huge crater. At 2072 metres I am slightly above Dome Shelter, looking down into steaming Crater Lake, which is surrounded by ice-cliffs, snow-fields and old lava flows.

Atop Ruapehu on this dazzlingly clear day, I can't help but feel a niggling sadness that the mountain has been debased by chairlifts, dynamited ski runs, chalets and ski villages. It has been turned into a commercial 'snowmanship' playground, when the original intention of the Maori chief in offering the volcanoes as a gift was that they be turned into a national park, to preserve their *mana*.

WHANGANUI NATIONAL PARK

I am picked up by a tour outfitter to canoe down the Whanganui River. DOC market it as the Whanganui Journey, one of New Zealand's nine 'Great Walks', although strictly speaking it is not a walk at all. The Whanganui River was the historical route to the interior, transporting goods and people until the railway and then the road were constructed.

'See ya down the river in three days,' says the outfitter. He drives his beat-up old van off in a cloud of dust, the empty trailer bouncing wildly behind. The colour of the river is industrial-strength grey, although it is in fact the black volcanic sand that lends it an opaque shade, and not pollution. It runs through a deep gorge of soft sandstone and mudstone formed from the ocean bed. In places, seashell fossils protrude from the sediments. The river has cut through this landscape with a dramatic flourish; as I drift dreamily downstream, waterfalls trickle down marble-smooth rock faces, and caves or hidden entrances to side rivers and creeks appear unexpectedly. Harder boulders stick out like chocolate chips in the crumbling biscuit of bedrock. A fluffy dandelion seed wafts by, cartwheeling so gently that the delicate grain dances on the surface of the river without getting wet. I paddle quietly, enjoying the scenery until some seven hours and several rapids later I reach John Coull Hut.

There is an ominous sign posted outside the hut's door:

> Canoeists should stop and back-paddle to allow jet boats to overtake. Jet boats, especially when fully loaded, require full power for some distance to get up and plane after slowing down. Therefore, if possible, canoeists should travel in groups, rather than straggle out over some distance.

I would have assumed I had the right of way, being in a frailer, slower craft. Competing with jet boats defeats the whole purpose of coming here.

The volunteer hut warden based here for the week engages me in conversation. He tells me he used to work as a labourer in Britain, before coming out to New Zealand with his wife when they were both still teenagers. By dint of hard work, they managed to save enough money to become dairy farmers, or 'cockies'. When they sold the farm, they bought a smaller property with the proceeds, to raise a small herd of beef cattle. Their annual one-week holiday is spent working as voluntary DOC hut wardens.

His shoulders are broad from decades of hard labour, his

forearms thick, his fingers gnarled and weather-beaten. He has not shaved for some days and a growth of white whiskers has sprouted on his ruddy cheeks. I ask him about the Maori village that Meri had mentioned.

He tells me: 'It's downstream. You can go down there and talk to them, if you want your ears buzzed off. They are friendly enough though, they'll tell you their side of the story.' He measures his words carefully; he is here as a voluntary hut warden and an ambassador for his adopted country. His wife watches expressionlessly and serves him a thick steak.

He tells me: 'The Whanganui is the largest continuously navigable river in New Zealand. The first settlement on the river was about 1350 AD, when people known as Te Atihau nui a papa rangi drifted into the valley, using the river as the route between coast and interior.'

Cutting into the slab of fresh beef as he talks, he also tells me about returning Kiwi soldiers from the First World War. They were granted land downstream along the Mangapurua branch of the river where the famous 'Bridge to Nowhere' crosses a deep chasm. His face and voice reflect both the pride and empathy he feels for the pioneer families who toiled to tame the bush, only to give up some twenty years later, broken and still owing the government money. He adds: 'Now, you can't see any evidence of the blood, sweat and tears those families shed to make a living there. It's all taken over by bush.'

I walk down to the riverbank. The sun sets and the moon, almost full, peers over the ridge of tangled vegetation high over the river. A morepork cries spookily, like a *kaitaiki*, a guardian spirit left behind by Maori ancestors at sacred places along the river. I retreat to the safety of the hut, just in case it *is* the warning cry of a Maori security goblin.

Next day the steep-sided river valley is thick with fog. I pack and launch my canoe into the swirling vapours. By mid-morning, the sun has burnt off the mist and soon the river valley becomes an unbearably hot cauldron. Downstream, a hidden entrance to the Tangarakau River provides a welcome diversion with the shade of overhanging vegetation. I paddle up its torpid waters, the river-bank thick with podocarps, palms and ferns, like a tunnel through tropical jungle. Even the tree trunks are covered with green para-sitic plants; I could imagine myself in Borneo, the Amazon or Africa, except there are no indigenous wild animals, just some exotic possums or feral goats, deer, pigs, cats and dogs. It is sur-prising how little bird life is here too, apart from the ubiquitous tui calling out like a familiar friend.

As I float by, a blast of cold air blows over me from a narrow slit, only a metre wide, opening to a deep and secret cavern. I back-paddle against the current and within the crevice catch a glimpse of a concealed world. Water has eroded a church-sized chamber, maybe fifty metres in diameter, crowded with ferns, palms, pools and waterfalls. Sunlight barely filters through the lush canopy above. I hold onto the rocks and stop to peer into this concealed biosphere.

Reaching Mangapurua side stream, I tie the canoe to a steel spike hammered into the soft ground and clamber up onto steps dug into the mudstone. A thirty-minute walk along a wide path-way, through a burrow of vegetation, brings me to the famous 'Bridge to Nowhere'. The massive concrete bridge, with its dizzying, hundred-metre drop to the Mangapurua River below, is now almost entirely disguised by encroaching vegetation. Its ram-parts are crumbling, and the only evidence of the abandoned farms, so laboriously carved out of the bush, are remnants of stone hearths. Lush green palm trees have been the first to reclaim the cleared pasture.

I had thought it strange that Kiwis displayed such reverence when discussing this bridge. It occurs to me, though, that it is not the bridge itself which is important. The bridge is simply sym-bolic evidence of the wasted lives of those settlers who did not succeed in taming the bush. Rural New Zealanders relate to that.

Uncut tall black beech, mixed with podocarp forest, dominate the ridge tops. Beside the path lies a plough, with the words 'Made in England' embossed in the rusty metal, and I imagine the farmers, their wives and their children walking along this same footpath. By 1942, the last of the war veterans who had tried to cultivate this isolated bush finally gave up. The Whanganui River had ceased to be a main transportation artery by the late nineteen-twenties, although boats still plied the river until the fifties. The most poignant reminders of these failed settlers are the colourful introduced flowers flourishing along the path edge.

Not much later, I hear the throaty roar of a jet boat echoing down the steep sides of the river, minutes before it catches up to me. I hug one side of the canyon as the machine hurtles by. None of the passengers, nor even the boat's driver, returns my wave. After the boat passes, I am left gripping the gunwales and balancing the canoe precariously while it is thrown about in the jet-boat's wake.

My first sight of Tieke Marae is tarpaulins stretched over wooden poles, giving the Maori village the air of a squatter's camp. Unsure of what to expect, I paddle the canoe onto the beach. As I pull the boat onto the sandbank, a young Maori boy blows on a conch shell. He descends and asks me to follow him through a semi-permanent archway of ferns.

As we walk, he tells me a little of the *marae*'s history. 'This used to be one of our old *pas*, where our tribal group built forti-fied villages. That is why I blew the *putorino*, the conch shell, to warn my people of your arrival. When the road was built to the east, our people moved away from the river and the ancient *pas*, to the activity and jobs along the road. The government declared this land public domain, which was good because it stopped set-tlers from cutting trees or developing the area. But the land was never bought from our people, and when DOC turned it into a national park, they did not have the right to do so.'

He pauses to take a breath, underlining the gravity of the mes-sage. 'We have come back to establish our rights. That is why we are here, why we have taken over the DOC hut and made it our *marae*. This *marae* is a symbol of our tribal identity and solidarity.'

'What is a *marae* anyway?' I ask, following him further up the slope.

The boy turns to face me proudly. 'Before, the *marae* meant the open area of land directly in front of the sacred carved home. Now a *marae* means all community buildings belonging to the tribe, not just the sacred house.' He formally warns me: 'You may not take alcohol, drugs or firearms on this *marae*. I will take you to the *powhiri*, welcome. As a *manuhiri*, visitor, you should follow me, then sit down where I show you and someone will sing for you. Then someone will speak and other men will perform a song. Then you must say who you are, where you are from, what you are doing here.'

He leads me to the open door of a former DOC hut, where a Maori flag is nailed to an outer wall. A huge plastic tarpaulin has been added to one side of the hut to partition off a kitchen and dining area. Makeshift wooden shelves are stacked with food. Mugs and cooking utensils hang from nails in the rafters. At the back of the kitchen is an open fireplace and two enormous smoke-blackened pots sit over the open flames.

I sit where I am told and the young man takes his place beside me to explain what is happening. A woman sings a high-pitched *karanga*, or welcome song, to arouse the spirits who have passed on to the spirit world. Then a young Maori, with freckles and dreadlocks, tatty trousers and a torn windbreaker, speaks in his native tongue. It is a melodious language, with much repetition of syllables. For the first time in New Zealand, I feel as if I am in a 'foreign' country. 'I shall translate now into my second language,' he says with pride. 'So that you understand.'

He repeats his message in English, welcoming me, telling the guardians, spirits and ancestors who I am. Two other young men join him. One has a broken nose and several of his teeth are missing. The other has Asian features with long, flowing black hair and traditional tattoos on his face. The men stand in front of me, their legs apart, knees bent. In perfect unison, they perform a *haka*, a fierce, war-like song which is accompanied by aggressive stamping of feet, loud slapping of thighs, punching of the air and hand gestures which remind me of karate chops. Then, holding their bodies still, their vertically held hands and fingers begin to quiver. At the end of a sequence of *wero*, ritual challenges, they pull their faces taut, eyes wide, tongues extended.

Despite the fearsome performance, they all line up afterwards to shake hands and offer me the traditional *hongi*, pressing their noses and foreheads against mine. First, the children extend this greeting, then the women, young men and finally the clan's patriarch. I feel as if I have been welcomed into a family.

Most of the narrow bunk beds in the DOC hut have been stripped of their mattresses, which have been laid alongside one another on the floor to make double beds. Family photographs adorn the walls. The few belongings are stuffed into plastic bags and hang from protruding nails. I feel like an intruder as I walk through this improvised 'bedroom' to the back of the hut, where I find a solitary empty bunk with its mattress.

It is getting dark. Outside, a young Maori boy in a woollen hat strums a guitar. A group of women talk and prepare vegetables for dinner.

I sit with Gay, a schoolteacher from Auckland. She tells me: 'My great-grandmother, Tauwiri Cribb, is about to have her gravesite unveiled the day after tomorrow, in a formal unveiling called *huru kohatu*. Some sixty tribe members are invited to attend the re-internment, or *hui*. Her body, which had been buried in the town of Wanganui, was disinterred a year ago and the remains brought up here to be buried on the site of the old *pa*.'

'Your great grandmother had an English surname?' I enquire.

'She married an Englishman, Cribb. He was a land surveyor.'

'That was a good move on his part, marrying a Maori chief's daughter.'

'I think it was her father who suggested it. He was smart. He used his son-in-law to manipulate the British laws to get land too.' She laughs, but I detect bitterness. 'That's what this is all about. Land.' She indicates with her dark eyes the hut, the tarpaulins and the ground. 'We have reoccupied our land.' Her face is determined, reflecting the passion she feels for this cause. 'We never gave it away or sold it.'

'And DOC?' I ask again.

'They are irrelevant now,' she says disparagingly. 'See some of these Maori boys? Many of our *rangatahi*, our young generation, have been in trouble in the cities. They have been disenfranchised. The Maori social structure has been completely fragmented by modern pakeha society. The pakeha represent almost 80 per cent of New Zealand's population, the Maori only 13 per cent. Even the Pacific Island Polynesians are 5 per cent. Now we bring our young people who are in trouble out here to learn the old Maori ways. Some have been here for over a year now and they don't want to leave.' Despite their fierce expressions whilst performing the *haka*, the tattoos, dreadlocks and broken, discoloured teeth, the teenagers seem warm, sincere and, most importantly, proud of their Maori identity. 'We get them sent to us from all over, often problem boys who run away from detention centres.' She laughs. 'Here there is nowhere to run to. To get through all that bush you'd have to be a good walker.'

'Who is in charge here?'

She points to the man hunched over by the fire. 'Mark Cribb, our chief, used to be.' The older man is talking with two other elders. 'He's the grandson of the land surveyor.'

'He doesn't live here any more?'

'Nah, he's moved back to Raetihi, but he comes back down here occasionally.' She talks with her hands, eyes and eyebrows, in the same way that Meri at the Ketetahi Hut did.

A young man sits down next to me. He wears a red T-shirt with the slogan: 'Death before Defeat'. He immediately dominates the conversation. Gay says nothing. When I ask questions about the Maori, he replies, with a twitch: 'I don't know. Ask my uncle' – pointing at the old man, Mark. 'He is our *kaumatua*, the keeper of the knowledge and traditions of the tribe. He knows about those political things.'

I ask him: 'Do you know about Te Heuheu's gift of land to the government to create Tongariro National Park?'

'No,' he replies, taken off guard by my question. Then he adds brusquely: 'Where'd you get your information from?'

'From the visitor centre at Whakapapa,' I reply defensively.

'Written by pakeha?'

'I don't know.'

'Pakeha don't know nothing. They write books about Maori things in English.'

'I'm not choosing to hear pakeha versions, all I'm trying to do is learn about the history of the area,' I reply, already feeling antipathy towards this man.

'Yeah, from pakeha,' he exclaims scornfully. 'How can they know about Maori things when they can't even speak our language?'

It is impossible to continue the discussion, so when he again refers to Mark as the guardian of the *marae*, I use this as an excuse to go and talk to the old chief. Mark speaks quietly and I have to strain to catch his words. He talks about the wildlife and the abundance of fish and birds when he was a boy. When I remark on the sparse bird life along the river, he replies: 'DOC drops 1080 poison by helicopter over the river. It kills the possums but it kills the birds as well. They admit 1080 kills some birds, but claims it is less than the damage created by possums eating eggs and chicks.' He shakes his head sadly. 'But the 1080 is killing them. There are no birds left here.' His eyelids droop, adding to his sad appearance.

Mark relates how the Maori took over the DOC hut almost four years ago. 'Within weeks of us squatting on this site, the police came to remove us, delivering a letter from the Minister of Justice. Our response was: "Take us to court. We're not moving out." Then they did their research, and they found out the government had no legal case to remove us.' He pauses proudly to let that bit of information sink in. 'We had done *our* research. Although our people moved away from the river decades ago to communities along the new road, which became our lifeblood instead of the river, we hadn't given up our rights to the old *pas* on the river. The government had unilaterally proclaimed the land a national park, but they had no legal right to do that. This is something that has happened to the Maori all over the country. The government backed off when they realised their mistake. Now DOC has had to incorporate our *marae*' – he spreads his hands wide, indicating the tarpaulins and tents – 'in their literature on the Whanganui National Park, which is mostly on Maori land anyway. Now there's a sort of truce between DOC and our people who "occupy" the government hut, which in turn occupied a traditional site of a Maori *pa* and *marae*.' He is silent. Deep creases line his weathered face as he stares at the flames of the cooking fire.

'Now you've established your rights on this site, where do you go from here?' I ask.

He takes a deep breath: 'Do the same thing up and down the river. Already there is another *marae*, the one you went by soon after John Coull Hut. Eventually we will have jurisdiction over the whole park again.'

Dinner is ready and as a guest, a *manuhiri*, I am told to start. There is an abundance of food: pots full of cauliflower with cheese sauce, cabbage, mashed potatoes, slices of corned beef and some kind of stew.

Mark gives the blessing and we all help ourselves.

Later in the evening, although there is no formal *paepae*, the place where the male elders sit in ceremonial gatherings, Mark stands in front of the fire and speaks softly and slowly, with authority. As the *kaumatua*, he is the last speaker. He prays, in Maori, pointing a stick at the hills, mountains, sky and river. His lined face is lit by pressure lanterns; he closes his eyes when he prays in Maori, but when he prays in English, he opens them and looks heavenward. Then he formally introduces himself, talks about the long white cloud, and also his lineage. He boasts about working on the riverboats for decades, as a deckhand. 'It is good to be back,' he concludes.

Each of us in turn stands up to introduce ourselves, to tell of our *whakapapa*, genealogy. The young ones from Auckland are not so sure of their own lineage. When it comes to my turn, I tell them: 'My father's father was Scottish and my father's mother was French. My mother's mother was Irish, and my mother's father was English. They migrated to Canada where I was born but we left when I was three. I lived in Asia and Africa until I went to university in Canada and France. Now my family live in Bermuda, England and Canada, but I have been living in my adopted country Norway, until now. Like you, I am also searching for my roots.' No wonder.

The young Maori with the woollen hat stands up. He takes off his cap, nervously wringing it in his hands. Gay whispers to me: 'He has been here only two days. Some of the Maori boys from the city have so little self-confidence and self-esteem they can't stand up in front of everyone and say their names in a meeting like this, even after several weeks. It is an emotional experience for me to see them regain some of their pride and self-respect.' The boy tells us his name, Sonny, and describes his *waka*, or canoe and his lineage. 'And that's all I have to say,' he concludes.

Then the young men do their fierce *haka* again, but it's slightly different from before. There are half a dozen Maori boys this time; one is unsure of the moves and keeps a watchful eye on the others as they go through their routines, mimicking them a split second too late. Despite his hesitant steps, he appears proud to re-enact this traditional Maori custom. Although the young men are dressed in rags and are barefoot, what they lack in costumes, they more than make up for in enthusiasm.

Mark thanks everyone again and then he leads us in *karakia*, a prayer, mostly in Maori, addressed to the gods who reside in the spirit world.

In the morning, after a huge breakfast, Murray, a big man with tattooed face and arms, dries the dishes with me. He tenderly holds a tiny baby in the crook of his arm, his biceps as big as the baby. The sides of his scalp are shaved, the remains of his long black hair are pulled back in a ponytail and his teeth are discoloured or missing.

'Too bad you start off looking so beautiful when you're young and end up being so ugly when you're older,' I joke.

He moves the baby from the crook of one arm to the other. 'Let me tell you a story. A Maori was in Europe visiting a friend and they walked past a monkey-grinder. You know, a man with an organ, and a monkey sitting on his shoulder. The Maori throws some money at them. "Why'd you do that?" his mate asks him. "I thought you didn't like the pakeha?" The Maori replies, "I don't like the pakeha, but their kids sure are cute." '

As a visitor, I must initiate the *poroporoaki*, or farewell. I contribute a *koha*, a donation of money and food to the *marae*, in return for their *manaaki*, or hospitality. Mark thanks me for visiting. Everyone accompanies me to the river edge and waves as I paddle away. Someone blows a conch horn, the plaintive notes echoing long after my departure.

Canoeing downstream, I pass three inflatable rafts pulled up on the beach beside pitched tents. White men, women and children are spread out on the shore or swimming in the river. One of them shouts generously: 'Want a tinnie, mate?'

Resting the paddle on the gunwales of the canoe, I reach out for the can of cold beer. As I drift downstream I ask: 'Hey, did you stop at Tieke Marae?' I swing my thumb over my shoulder, pointing to where I have just come from. It's been a highlight of my trip to New Zealand staying at the *marae*, talking to the Maori, trying to understand where they are coming from.

'No bloody way!' a big man with a fiery red beard bellows back at me angrily.

NATIONAL PARK – TAUPO – ROTORUA

When I return to National Park, Peter, the owner of the backpackers, invites me to accompany him and his son Paul to Feilding, to watch the car races. Although it is a weekend and their lodge is full, this regular summer excursion to the Sunday races is an activity not to be missed.

At the stadium in Feilding, we sit behind half a dozen men who have staked out their turf in the stands, sitting on a bench seat of a car, covered with sheepskin. They cook sausages and bacon on a portable barbeque, resting their feet on a couple of 'chilly bin' coolers, from which they occasionally extract beer.

Formula Vees, flea-like versions of Formula One cars powered by Volkswagen engines, accelerate down the track. At the first turn, cars clash and a cloud of bluish smoke explodes. In the aftermath four Vees lie squashed on the track. The race is a demolition derby, cars all over the place, at times more off the track than on. What the drivers lack in skill, they make up for in determination, yet the Vee jockeys are nothing compared to the Mad Max Mazda RX-7 drivers who follow them. In the first turn, half a dozen Mazdas are left battered and bent, but amazingly the drivers all manage to get back in the race.

'It's doorhandle to doorhandle stuff out there,' the commentator says. 'Going into the straight, it's bumper-to-bumper action as the express train comes through to the second turn.' Two more cars spin out at the bend, one rolling onto its roof. 'There's two more in the kitty litter and it looks like one has fallen over.'

The commentator also reminds the audience which island, the North or the South, each of the contestants is from. The sponsorship of these cars is varied: 'Romena's Massage Lounge' has an enticing paint job of two naked women on the bonnet, both of them now with their shapely legs crushed out of shape. Besides Romena's massages, there are other equally appropriate sponsors, including 'Foxton Body Parts', 'Academy Funeral Services' and 'Prestige Smash Repairs'. 'Robb's Fruits and Vegies' seems less appropriate, unless the fruits and vegies are the drivers.

At the end, the winner climbs onto the stand. He says he is 'rapt' about winning, and that is the extent of his acceptance speech. He collects a bottle of champagne as a prize, opens it and splashes it around before drinking what is left. Then he gets into his crumpled car and they both gurgle and belch back to the pits.

We buy huge hot dogs covered in batter and fried in oil, then dipped in tomato sauce. A big man, with tattoo-covered arms and flowing beard, turns to face the stands behind him and makes a big show of lifting up his black tank top to expose a very white, very rotund, furry-red belly. He puts his hands under it for leverage and shakes it up and down, proud of its jelly-like mass.

'Come on!' a woman behind me yells enthusiastically into my ear. 'Take it all off! Don't be a girl!'

In the morning, while sitting in one of the spotless toilets at the backpackers lodge in National Park, I discover too late that there is no toilet paper. I wait patiently, hoping someone will come along so I can ask them to hand me a roll from one of the other cubicles. Twenty long minutes later, finally giving up on being rescued, I shamble forward in the sitting position to slide the bolt and surreptitiously open the door of the cubicle. There is no one else in the toilet. I pull the door wide open and continue cautiously, still crouched, with shorts and underpants wrapped snugly around my ankles, shirt tail hoisted clear of my bare ass. I am totally out of the cubicle, bent over, about to shuffle sideways to the adjacent cubicle, when Wilma the cleaner walks in. I freeze and we both stare at each other. I shuffle sideways and backwards into the toilet cubicle, like a retreating hermit crab, but in my haste I trip over the tangle of clothes binding my feet together. I collapse on my naked bum, head pressed hard against the porcelain toilet bowl, and kick the door shut with both feet.

'Need some toilet paper?' Wilma asks, correctly assessing my plight.

'Ah yuh,' I reply, from my prone position, screwing up the Kiwi pronunciation yet again.

Wilma's hand reaches discreetly under the door with a roll of toilet paper. 'By the way,' she says, deadpan, 'this is the ladies.'

Later, discreetly ignoring our earlier encounter, Wilma tells me she is driving into Taupo with her husband, Lani. I catch a ride with them. Although I have seen Wilma working every day cleaning the lodge, I have not had a chance to talk to her. She sits with their son Didi in the back seat of their big four-wheel drive.

'I'm employed at the local sawmill as a supervisor,' Lani tells me. 'I'm a Maori from the north, while Wilma is a Maori from this area.'

Driving along the two-lane highway, we pass the Englishman walking along the side of the road, on his way from Invercargill to Cape Reinga. Why would anyone do that to himself? I turn in my seat to look at him again. His face is determined, eyes focused on the ground in front of his feet.

'Shall I pick him up?' Lani asks.

'Uh-uh,' I reply, shaking my head. 'He's walking all the way from Invercargill up to Cape Reinga. He doesn't take short-cuts or lifts. He's going to walk every step of the way.'

I admire his determination, but have to wonder what drives him.

Wilma leans forward from the back seat and asks: 'Do you mind if we call you by the Maori equivalent of your name?'

'Sure, no problem.'

She tells me: 'Anaru, we spent yesterday with Sir Hepe Te Heuheu, now seventy-nine years old, and the direct descendant of Horonuku Te Heuheu Turkino, who donated the volcano summits to the British Crown. Did you climb the volcanoes?'

'Yes.'

'What did you think?'

'I was disappointed.'

Lani, a huge man with fists the size of bear paws, looks over at me. He asks, in a deep voice that seems almost to echo in his chest, 'Why? Bad weather?'

'No, I had beautiful weather, just like today. That was probably part of the problem. Tongariro was swarming with close to a thousand trampers. It's hard to get a sense of the *tapu* and *mana* of the volcano when there are so many people around. The next day on Ruapehu, a chairlift took me most of the way up the mountain. Doesn't exactly instil a sense of awe. It is sad to see the park desecrated by chairlifts, dynamited slopes and sculpted ski fields. There's no sense of sacredness, or power.'

Lani's eyes widen as he listens.

I continue without any prompting, giving vent to my feelings: 'I'd close all those ski resorts down and make the mountain a holy place again. Maybe the mountain agrees, maybe that's why it keeps blowing its top. It's hardly my place to say this, but even as a visiting tourist, I get upset seeing the obvious exploitation of the volcanoes, especially when I learnt why they were gifted as national parks in the first place. But I guess there is too much money invested now to turn it all back.'

I'm not exactly an unprejudiced observer. I have a reconstructed knee from a ski accident many years ago, and haven't downhill-skied since that mishap. I have no wish to, either.

Lani has been quiet but he cannot restrain himself any longer. He says: 'We laughed with joy when the mountain erupted last year and the year before, as if the spirits of the volcanoes were telling us something.'

He turns the radio off, although the music was barely audible. 'You know, when a tramper dies on the volcanoes, it's business as usual with DOC. They don't close the mountain down in respect for the deceased. That is not the Maori way. For us, there has to be a decontamination process.'

Wilma says earnestly: 'We look upon the mountains with reverence. *Te ha o Taku Manawa*. The breath of my mountain is my heart. We are proud they were given to the nation, whose people, being nature-lovers, should accord them respect. Maori respect for the mountains goes deep. In our genealogies, all life originated from the same parents, Papa the earth-mother and Rangi the sky-father, so that man and all life forms are in harmony with one another, in the bonds of kinship. We look upon those volcanoes as ancestors, and this relationship is also a reminder of our forefathers who settled in the mountains' shadows centuries ago. In these memories the past and present mingle, ensuring continuity. That is why we pay the mountains homage.'

Both Wilma and Lani are movingly eloquent on the subject of Maori history.

Wilma continues. 'Our people want to go back to the feet of the mountain, as part of relearning our Maori way. But we are not sure how to approach Tongariro now; it is difficult to know which way is right any more. We organised a bus trip some time ago and some of our elders were not keen on going because of the *tapu*. Others did not want to go far up the mountain. You must understand that although most of us are Christians, we have not forgotten our Maori ways. The ladies on the bus, they recited Maori prayers. For some it was the first time they had been in the park, although they have lived near Taumarunui or Turangi most of their lives. This matter of *tapu* is important. We want people to enjoy the mountain but we do not want it desecrated. Some of our people feel more strongly than others. Some do not want commercialism on the mountains at all; to others it is no problem because it is the pakeha doing the skiing anyway. The *tapu* is still there, but it is no longer the kind that kills. The gift was a Maori–pakeha thing, and we want it to stay that way, but the commercialism is dividing our community.'

Lani adds: 'When our ancestors, the first Polynesians, arrived here in New Zealand, they found a rich and empty land. As they settled, one tribe would confront another in the search for good agricultural land. Warfare became a way of life, although the fights were mostly small and often only ended in injuries. Before the pakeha arrived, the whole of Maori culture, from song and dance, to the choice of leaders and living places, depended on the culture of war. War was the highest inspiration, but it was limited because of the crudeness of our weapons.' He glances at me. 'You've heard of the Treaty of Waitangi?'

I nod.

He glances back at the road, his massive fingers curled around the padded steering wheel. 'At that time the Bay of Islands was a den of sin. European sailors, loggers, deserters, criminals – all were corrupting the local Maori, trading muskets for land, taking our women. Then when there was total disorder and lawlessness, the British authorities persuaded a few of the Maori chiefs in the area to ask the British for protection, from the whites as much as the Maori, who went on the rampage with newly acquired British muskets. With this bit of paper, which they called the Waitangi Treaty, the British went over the whole country and confiscated any land belonging to Maori who didn't recognise British sovereignty.' He laughs with irony. 'Can you imagine it, the Treaty of Waitangi was signed by thirty-nine Maori chiefs around the Bay of Islands area, yet that piece of paper gave the British monarch sovereignty over all of New Zealand! Most of the Maori didn't understand English anyway.'

Lani is facing the windscreen, but that does not reduce the intensity of his words: 'A minister of the church translated the original English treaty but he couldn't properly translate the text into Maori. Five hundred Maori chiefs eventually signed that document, but the Maori version ceded only the right to govern, not the Maori's right to chieftainship. In any case, the treaty had no legal basis.' He turns to look at me, emphasising the point. 'No basis in legality whatsoever.' He stares at the road in front of us again, driving slowly, in no rush to get to Taupo. 'Imagine if Japan invaded pakeha New Zealand now, imposing their own laws and religion and confiscating land if anyone rebelled against them, and then they resettled Japanese immigrants on the confiscated land . . . Imagine how the pakeha would react.'

He pauses, and I think about what he has said. Then, with a glance at the volcanoes, he returns to the subject of our earlier discussion: 'There's no doubt in my mind that those ski fields will no longer exist in the future. The ski chalets will go, the chairlifts, the shops and the cafés. The volcano still has its *mana*, it'll destroy everything, maybe not now, maybe not even in our lifetimes, which is nothing for a volcano. But eventually all the man-made stuff will disappear.'

'And the income?'

'And the income.' He shrugs. 'That's been the problem: money and greed. But the *mana* and the *tapu* of the mountain will have been preserved and that is more important.'' He turns to his wife. 'All these things will come about, the changes will be made.' She nods in agreement. 'All this land here' – he indicates with a sweeping motion of his hand as we pass the volcanoes on our right – 'belongs to us. It will come back to us.'

'You must be kidding? Given back to you? All the land around the park, or the national park itself?' I find it hard to share his belief.

'Mostly the park.'

'Are you sure?'

He laughs: 'I am very sure. It may take time, but that is also the Maori way. Real Maori are patient. A year, many years, mean nothing.' In many ways Lani reminds me of a North American Indian, but it seems to me the Maori have a lot more reason for optimism than do the aboriginal peoples almost anywhere else in the colonised world. They have become a lot more integrated into the mainstream, without necessarily losing their culture or identity. 'The land will come back to us, I know. It will all fall into place. Maori believe; we have faith that things will always work out. It is our tradition.'

'When you get all that land back, with all that power, it's going to open a whole new can of worms.'

He laughs: 'Yeah. Too true.'

'Then it will be all about money and greed again, except this time it will be in the hands of Maori, not pakeha.'

'True.'

As we drive over the crest of a hill, we can see Lake Taupo in front of us.

I break the ensuing silence by telling them about my canoeing on the Whanganui. 'I was impressed with the Maori occupying the old *pa* at Tieke Marae.' Lani knows it well and knows Mark Cribb too. 'A precedent has been set,' I continue. 'It was great to see the reoccupation happen successfully, but I have my doubts in the long term.'

'Why?' Lani asks, looking at me again.

'Mark Cribb is an elder and it was easy to talk to him. He's conciliatory, he believes Maori and pakeha are all Kiwis. The land issue is just redressing some of the old imbalances. The young Maori boy who, I was told, will succeed him, is a real firebrand and it didn't seem to me that he had any use for the pakeha at all.'

Lani nods pensively and stares out the window. Two cyclists pedalling the other way work hard to climb up the long hill. He waves at them. 'We have a lot of problems with young Maori who don't know their own history or culture, shouting down elders, being too radical. But Greenpeace had to be radical to get people to pay attention, so I am not sure that it is all so bad. Anyway, the youth all over the world are often angry and ignorant, not just the Maori. But yes, when they don't know their own history, when they aren't patient, don't listen, don't do things by consensus, then they are not acting in the Maori tradition.' He shakes his head. 'Many urban Maori have never been to a *marae*. Many have almost no contact with their cultural roots. That is bad.' He takes his hand off the steering wheel to emphasise his point. 'But I am sure that young man will learn. Just by being there, he will learn about his people's history. Even talking to visitors like you will help him to understand what he doesn't know. It's not so hopeless. He can't stay ignorant forever.'

I like Lani's ability to see the positive side to things.

'You did the *hongi* greeting?' Wilma asks from the back seat. 'Yes.'

'You know why they rub noses?' Lani questions.

'To share the breath of life?' I reply.

'No, that's what everyone thinks, even many Maori. Originally it wasn't the touching of noses at all, it was the touching of foreheads.' He pats his forehead for emphasis. 'The noses just touched by coincidence.'

'What was the symbolism in touching foreheads?'

'The exchange of knowledge. For the Maori, the head was *tapu*. At ceremonies the heads of ancestors would be brought out, as if they were still alive, to add their wisdom. It has nothing to do with the touching of noses.'

'All the guidebooks I've seen say it's the sharing of the breath of life.'

'That's wrong, and I am sure of it.' He places a hand on his head again. 'Traditionally, it was the touching of foreheads as a symbolic exchange of knowledge.'

He pulls off the road at a point overlooking Lake Taupo and switches off the ignition. 'You know, Lake Taupo is one of the world's largest active volcanoes. When it erupted in 186 AD, creating this lake, it was one of the most violent eruptions ever.'

He moves his outstretched palm in a semi-circle. 'The land before you is important in Maori culture. Traditionally, tribal occupation of an area had to be defended against other tribes. That was how a particular tribe held communal rights over that land. There was no "individual ownership", as we know it today. European law undermined this traditional relationship, by imposing individual title and rights. It was because of this that Horonuku Te Heuheu Tukino gave his "gift" of the volcanoes. It was a final attempt to prevent the pakeha from taking everything we had.'

We get out of the vehicle. Didi stays in the back, reading. Lani points behind us at the volcano. 'Mananui Te Heuheu Tukino II's bones were brought up the slopes of Tongariro to be buried there, to strengthen the claim of ownership of his tribe, the Ngati Tuwharetoa. He had become paramount chief because of his ability to lead and defend his people against tribes encroaching from the north, equipped with muskets obtained from the pakeha. When he successfully defended Ngati Tuwharetoa occupation of land in the Taupo–Tongariro area, he became the most influential and powerful leader in the interior of the North Island,' Lani says proudly. I could easily imagine Lani himself as a paramount chief. 'He was one of the principal Maori leaders who refused to put his mark to the Treaty of Waitangi.'

We walk over to the railing at the edge of the lookout point, and stare out at the huge volcanic caldera lake and rolling countryside all around us.

Lani continues his history lesson. 'The chief was killed in a landslide and succeeded by his brother, Iwikau Te Heuheu, just when Maori society was being destroyed by pressure for land sales from colonists, increase in diseases brought by the pakeha, and alcohol. To fight off any further colonisation here, the Maori reorganised themselves and accepted a Maori King, just as the British had a King, to lead them and stabilise internal Maori politics.' He lifts a foot to rest it on the guardrail. 'That is why this is called "King country", not because of the British king. The pakeha reacted to this threat by confiscating two million acres of "rebel" land.' He points to the west. 'That's Pukawa, where the Kingitangi Movement started. It was there that they decided to elect a Maori King.

'Then Horonuku Te Heuheu, son of Mananui Te Heuheu Tukino II, took over as paramount chief after the death of his uncle Iwikau. Ngati Tuwharetoa warriors took part in the battle at Orakau. Three hundred Maori men, women and children fought off eighteen hundred British troops equipped with cavalry and artillery. That was our last successful fight against the British. After this, our loss of land was completed during the Land Wars. Instead of dealing with tribes, the British Native Land Act required the Native Land Court to individualise Maori land tenure, making it even easier for land purchase agents to buy from individual Maori owners. We had to confront the European system of land law, which changed the entire historical basis of Maori land ownership.'

The sun beats down on us. Wilma fetches soft drinks from the car and hands them around. Lani continues: 'My grandfather used to tell me stories every night when I was a boy. When he was young, his father told him how the first pakeha, outnumbered by Maori, stayed in New Zealand on our terms. Then more traders, whalers, sealers and loggers arrived. Those early ties with the pakeha were increased and the balance was gone.' He takes a drink before continuing. 'Bit by bit, our Maori culture was lost. The traders slowly destroyed our society, especially with the changes brought about by the musket. The existing social balance among the Maori tribes disintegrated and the pakeha dominated, taking advantage of the new divisions among our people. That's why it was so easy to get weak Maori chiefs to sign the Treaty of Waitangi in 1840, setting Maori against Maori. Once the pakeha had the Treaty of Waitangi they used it to wipe out our people's resistance. We had a choice: accept the pakeha way, or be destroyed. Sadly, Maori and pakeha cultures remain largely separate.'

He thinks for a while before turning to look at me, laughing. 'Look, it could be a lot worse. At least we're not totally dispossessed, like the Aborigines in Australia or the Indians in North or South America. Here in New Zealand, there has been a greater degree of integration of the indigenous people into the mainstream.' He reflects before adding: 'We have a lot to be grateful for now.'

He mulls that statement over for a while before continuing. 'You know, we have an adopted son, a pakeha. He was bothered that he wasn't dark-skinned like the Maori. One day when he was seven, he came home from school looking happy. He says to Wilma: "I know I am part Maori." ' Lani laughs, tears in his eyes. Wilma is smiling at the memory too. ' "How do you know?" Wilma asks him. "Because," our son replies, "I have brown freckles." '

We get back into the vehicle. Didi is still sitting in the back, reading.

'Does your adopted son still think he's a Maori?' I ask Lani.

Lani smiles. 'He is twenty-one now and he is as much a Maori as any Maori. Even legally, he is a Maori.' He turns around to ask Didi: 'Does your brother think he is a Maori?'

'Yeah,' Didi replies, looking up briefly from his book to answer. 'It wasn't his fault he wasn't born one.'

Lani starts the engine and we pull out onto the road. Out of nowhere, he asks me: 'How close are you to nature?'

I reflect before replying. It is hard to answer without sounding corny. 'Wherever I am, I don't really feel myself unless I am close to nature. Through nature, I commune with myself, feel at peace and reach a higher spiritual level. A bit like some people probably feel going into a church.' I look out the window as we drive over a bridge spanning a sparkling, turquoise river. 'Sometimes, here in New Zealand, I have reached a level of being close to nature quite unlike anything I've felt before. Your rainforests are so thick with vegetation it is sometimes impossible to see anything that is not green and alive. Something about it, some kind of earth energy, makes my body and my spirit react. I feel a surge of happiness, as if my body knows that this dense forest, which has been around long before humankind, is what gives me life. Here in New Zealand's nature there is nothing harmful to me, and I find myself in harmony. I always walk by myself, and sense this tranquillity within seconds of being in your bush.' I stare out at some of the most beautiful countryside I have ever witnessed.

'But you could easily vandalise what you've got here. You ruin the peacefulness of your nature with all those jet skis, jet boats, helicopters, planes, bungee jumping and flying foxes. You are very much like North Americans with their extreme sports. Perhaps my attitude is more that of a European, conserving a wilderness area as a haven of peace, rather than making it an adventure playground. I can see both perspectives, but personally, if I had a choice, I know what it would be.'

We continue skirting around the lake towards Taupo. It is midday and the wind bends the tall toitoi grass. The water of Lake Taupo is clear and flowing into it are some of the best trout rivers in the world. The snow-clad volcanic mountains serve as a backdrop, clearly visible at the other end of the lake. Taupo itself, the volcano, is not extinct. It is expected to blow again with blistering force.

Taupo the town is a hyperactive hive of adventure. We stop at an ice-cream parlour. Didi is wearing what Lani calls his arc-welder's mask, but it is in fact a pair of fashionable wrap-around sunglasses. He accepts an ice-cream cone and wanders off to the computer store.

I feel I have established a friendship with Lani and Wilma in the drive here from National Park. I tell them, sincerely: 'It's been one of the highlights of my trip to New Zealand to have talked with you.'

'Thanks for sharing your ideas with us. You've opened our eyes too, about jet boats and things. Maybe we need to reappraise our ideas about recreation and our environment,' Lani says, genuinely.

When it is time for my bus to leave it seems perfectly natural and proper that we part ways by a traditional *hongi*. We have just spent some hours sharing our knowledge and the symbolic clunking of foreheads represents that exchange. I board the bus and wave goodbye to Lani, Wilma and Didi. In the space of only a few short hours, I have felt very close to them; it surprises me the level at which we communicated. Alone on the bus, I miss them already.

⋙

Rotorua was founded in 1880 for Europeans to enjoy the healing thermal waters and the fabled pink and white terraces, later destroyed by a volcanic eruption. It has a certain charm despite ample evidence of a flourishing tourism industry. I ignore the up-market accommodation along Fenton Street and take a room at one of the backpacker lodges, which has its own natural hot-spring tub.

The next morning, on a backpackers' tourist bus, the driver/guide asks: 'Where you from?'

'Norway,' I reply, changing nationalities to suit my mood.

'Cool, sweet as,' he says. He puts the bus, which has seen better days, into gear and we take off.

'Welcome to Rotovegas, folks.' He tells us a joke to warm us up. 'A Kiwi goes to a farm in Australia and sees a sheep with its head stuck in the fence. The Kiwi comes up to the sheep from behind, and drops his pants and bang, bang, bang. Then the Kiwi turns to the Australian and says, "OK, now it's your turn." The Australian drops his pants and sticks his head in the fence.'

An Australian at the back of the bus yells: 'That's an Aussie joke about the Kiwis.'

'Ah yeah? Well here, mate, it's a Kiwi joke about the Aussies.'

'Bloody upstart Kiwis,' the Australian mutters, but loud enough so that half the bus can hear. 'They do their big OE to Australia and they think they've seen the world.'

As we pull into the sulphurous area of town, the distinct rotten-egg odour of the thermal springs infiltrates the bus. The driver tells us, undoubtedly repeating a standard gag: 'Rotorua is the only place in New Zealand where they thank you for farting.'

I am beginning to regret the decision to do the tourist thing. We are herded to Lady Knox geyser, which stands about two metres high, a perfect miniature volcano, exuding a trace of steam from the top. We wait expectantly, as if for the start of a TV show. A staff member dumps a kilo of soap bars down the geyser to break up the viscosity of the surface tension of the water table below. Within minutes, the geyser regurgitates suds; detergent perfumes the air as bubbles begin floating out of the opening. It performs like a trained circus animal, spouting steaming water ten metres into the air, right on cue. Then, suddenly, the show is over. The throng of tourists disappears, to board buses for the next scheduled natural attraction.

It's easy to see how New Zealanders can adopt an anti-nuclear stance: the country is rich in power sources with massive potential for both hydro and thermal energy. Between Taupo and Rotorua alone, there are several hundred hot springs which the Maori have used to cook food for centuries.

Out of idle curiosity, on my way to the backpackers lodge, I stop in at a gun shop. The man behind the counter asks: 'Can I help?'

I reply, 'How can I get a hunting licence?'

He blinks at me, his eyes magnified by thick glasses. 'You don't need a hunting licence. You get a firearm licence and then you can buy as many guns and hunt whatever you want.'

'So how do I get a firearm licence?'

'Ask your wife,' he says.

'Ask my wife?' I repeat.

'Yeah. Bloody ridiculous isn't it?' he says, warming to me despite the fact that I am a foreigner asking such basic questions.

'In this country, you ask your wife if you want to get a firearm licence.'

'What do you mean?'

'First, the police check to see if you've got a criminal record. Good on 'em. Now they also ask your wife if it's all right with her if you have a firearm licence. What's it to do with her if I've got a firearm licence? Well, ever since the battered housewives' law, your wife has to agree for you to get a firearm licence.' He blinks again, his blue eyes magnified out of all proportion to his face. It makes him look like an innocent cartoon character. He shakes his head. 'She has to agree in case she feels threatened. If she says no to you getting a licence, the police won't tell you why they refused you a licence, in case you beat the shit out of her.' He thumps a tiny hand on the counter. 'Bloody ridiculous, a man having to ask his wife for permission to get a gun. In Canada, Britain and even Australia, it's getting harder to get a firearm licence. It's a conspiracy. Did you know that?' I shake my head in amazement, which he interprets as commiseration. 'It's the bloody UN or something. I heard some women's group in the UN wants all privately owned firearms eliminated by the year 2000. They can't do that here. They don't know New Zealanders, if they think they can pull that one here. There'd be bloody civil war.'

'What do you mean?' I ask.

'Gun owners in New Zealand?' Blink. 'Hand their guns in to the police?' Blink. 'Fuck 'em.' Blink, blink. 'There'd be civil war here for sure. We'd fight for the right to have firearms.'

Faxes have been coming through on his fax machine. There is a *Soldier of Fortune* magazine behind the counter. The telephone rings. He answers it and I take advantage to slip out before he tries to recruit me to his cause. I signal to him with extended thumb to my ear and pinkie waggling by my mouth that I will phone him later when he is not so busy organising the revolution.

Ducking into a nearby bookshop, I browse through the Outdoors section. Several books have variations on the title: *Bringing Home the Bacon*. The authors pose carrying bloody pigs on their backs or kneeling proudly beside dead boars, whose mouths are held open with sticks to reveal pencil-thin tusks. There is a dreadful photo of a man astride a white-eyed, terrified hog, a dog pulling it by the bleeding nose and two more dogs chewing on its ears and hind legs. He is captured in black-and-white plunging a knife into the pig's side. A whole shelf of authors, men and women, show the rest of us how to bring home the bacon the tough way.

As I leave the bookstore, a small piece on the front page of the newspaper catches my eye:

MAN TAKES ON SHARK

An Invercargill man jumped off a boat and wrestled with a four-metre shark in Milford Sound yesterday. Grant Lightfoot was on a diving boat when the shark was sighted. Others on the boat went to look over the side at the thresher shark, but Mr Lightfoot jumped in and killed it with his knife. 'I don't know why I did it. It was a spur of the moment thing.' Mr Lightfoot plans to keep the jaw as a trophy.

What's with these guys?

FEBRUARY

LAKE WAIKAREMOANA

Riding in the front seat beside the bus driver to ward off motion sickness, I still feel pangs of nausea as we negotiate an endless series of turns, swinging into another bend before we have completed the previous one. You would think he was driving a Formula One car on a racetrack and not a bus on a gravel road. The front wheels are often dangerously close to a precipitous drop down steep cliffs into a river valley. Despite the driver's reassurance that he has driven this route for twenty years, I feel apprehensive. It would be my bad luck to be with him when his good luck runs out.

Hours later and much to my relief, we pull up at isolated Lake Waikaremoana. It is cold outside and grey clouds hang heavy in the sky. Judging from the open pack and unfurled sleeping-bag inside the spartan DOC bunkhouse, someone else is there to keep me company.

To shake out the stiffness in my joints from the bus ride, I walk down to the lake. A woman dives into the dark waters, swimming some distance before returning to climb up onto the pebbly beach. She sees me looking at her and smiles with a broad, toothy grin. Crow's feet spread from the outer corners of striking blue eyes. Her strong facial features hint at an equally resolute personality. Her hair is pulled up in a topknot, revealing the softness of the skin on the nape of her neck.

Ingrid, my bunkhouse-mate, introduces herself and extends her hand in greeting; her grip is firm. As we walk back to the bunkhouse together she tells me she has been driving around New Zealand in a second-hand car. She has a barely perceptible German accent.

'You just decided to take the year off and drive around New Zealand?' I ask, holding the bunkhouse door open for her.

'Yes,' Ingrid answers. She adds, hinting at some dark secret as she enters the cabin: 'I'm just taking it one day at a time. The headmaster of my school told me to take as much time as I need. I teach remedial kids.'

She talks about her pupils and laughs: 'I miss them.'

Ingrid puts the water on to boil to make tea, and changes out of her one-piece swimsuit into warmer clothes. She must be in her mid-thirties, but has the lean, muscular body of a much younger woman.

We sit outside on the doorstep, drinking herbal tea. Low, dense clouds obscure the sun. She recounts some of the highlights of her trip to New Zealand. 'I climbed Mount Aspiring and Mount Cook,' she says, matter-of-fact. 'I like climbing mountains. In Germany, we rode motorbikes all the time, my husband and I.' She hesitates momentarily, before continuing: 'We rode everywhere in Europe and did a lot of climbing. We climbed Mont Blanc, from the bottom up, using no lifts.'

She tries to warm herself against the outside chill, holding the mug tightly cupped in both hands. 'Some things happened here that made me really happy.' Her face is animated and full of vitality when she speaks. She has a child-like demeanour, emphasised by a barely disguised giggle as she relates her experiences. 'I was on Dusky Sound in Fiordland. We were several tourists in a boat after doing a dive and saw bottlenose dolphins swimming in the fiord. We put on wetsuits and jumped into the water.' Her excitement is infectious. 'One dolphin stayed to play with us. We formed a circle, holding hands, the dolphin swam up from underneath and jumped out of the water from within our circle. You can imagine our surprise. He did this several times, sometimes almost landing back on top of us. I touched him often. The dolphin seemed to like it, did not swim away and always came back, especially to me. The others climbed into the boat because they were so cold, but I stayed in the water. The dolphin was big and kept circling so close to me. It was too tempting not to, so I reached for his dorsal fin and he dragged me through the water. When I couldn't hold on any longer and let go, he came back, as if to pick me up and take me somewhere far away.' She laughs at the memory. 'He pulled me around for almost half an hour, returning many times if I let go. It was a wonderful, strange experience.'

For some time she is quiet and when I look at her I see she is crying. She wipes the tears from her eyes. 'Really, it is impossible to describe my feelings.' She continues: 'It happened again at Akaroa. I swam quite far out from the shore because I heard there were Hector dolphins there. I started to sing underwater. Maybe five or ten minutes later, six Hector dolphins came and played with me. When I was tired, I swam ashore. There were people watching me on shore and they told me the dolphins swam all the way with me, although I did not see them. That was magnificent, too.' She reflects for a while. 'In Abel Tasman, I rented a kayak for some days and several times seal pups climbed onto the kayak.'

It is almost sunset. Dark clouds break in the west, revealing a golden horizon. A breeze picks up, scooting white crests of waves down the lake. We take advantage of the clearer skies to go for a walk. Ingrid leads me up a well-used track through dense bush. The lake shimmers like molten gold, reflecting the colour of the sky. The bush is thick with ferns, vines and moss, but on the edge of the cliff the slanting rays of the sun cut under the canopy of vegetation. We reach a giant rata tree more than eight hundred years old, according to a sign at its base. Craning my neck to look up, I see two levels, floors of vegetation where you could build a substantial tree house.

The last rays of the sun filter through the vegetation. As the light fades, the forest rapidly becomes sinister and threatening.

Darkness embraces the gaps and clearings, and it is easy to imagine goblins amongst the shadows. I follow Ingrid's shadowy figure as we descend through the bush.

Back at the bunkhouse we prepare hot chocolate and, dressed warmly, escape the confines of the cabin. We sit outside by the lake again, watching the stars and looking for satellites. There doesn't seem to be as many satellites here as there are in the northern hemisphere. Sometimes we talk, often there is silence; but the stillness between us is comfortable. The breeze pushes waves onto the pebbly beach with gentle, invisible splashes.

'Where do you live?' she asks, turning to look at me. I hesitate. 'You don't know?' she prompts, misinterpreting my silence.

'I've been living in Norway for the last five years.'

'With someone?' she asks.

'Yes. That's why I moved there.'

'And she is still special?'

'Yes. I mean . . . I just don't know how to explain it exactly. Even though I have not seen her for some months and do not know when I will, or for how long, somehow I feel I still have her in my heart.'

'But you have left her, and Norway?'

'Officially, yes.'

'Unofficially?'

'Unofficially, as well.' I look over at her. It is not a very satisfactory answer, but it is an honest one.

'But why?'

I try to explain but my words seem inadequate.

She nods anyway, as if comprehending despite my tongue-tied justification for leaving behind someone that I love. 'And where will you go after New Zealand?'

'I don't honestly know yet. I just want to think about things for a while. Coming here, I am far away from everyone and have lots of time to think.'

'And heal.'

'Yes.' My monosyllabic reply is hardly a conversational gambit. It's funny, or perhaps not so funny, how us guys become unintelligible or mute when it comes to our feelings and emotions. Comes with the territory of being a male, I guess.

'And you, what happened to your marriage?' I ask, changing the focus. Let's see how she answers the same question.

'My husband died.'

Waves continue to lap on the shore, filling the breach in our conversation. She picks up a pebble, examines it carefully and then tosses it into the lake with a splash. 'So I too am here to heal.'

'I'm sorry,' I say, the response inadequate. We have not come here to escape reality so much as to grow again. If I wanted to I could turn the clock back and still return to a love I left behind. She cannot.

'It's OK. I came to New Zealand to get away and I have not talked about it for a while. Maybe it is good to do so, sometimes.' Her voice, just a whisper before, becomes stronger, the tone gentle and resigned.

'How long ago?' I turn to her. Even in the darkness, I see the girlish look on her face has gone. She seems tired now.

'A year ago.' Her fingers are locked together and she studies the backs of her hands. She takes a deep breath. The waves ripple on the shore. It seems as if she is silent for a long time, although it is probably only minutes before she continues, her voice less steady, her emotions barely in check: 'I took a month off teaching after he died. We had met there at the school. He was the children's bus driver. We were married for nine years.'

She pauses. The night air suddenly grows colder and I shiver.

She perseveres, her voice small, as if she were far away. 'We were riding our motorbikes, not far from home in Germany. I was behind. An old man in a car pulled out into the road. My husband accelerated, trying to go around, but the old man tried to drive out of the way across the road. My husband crashed into the car.'

A morepork's lament disturbs the rhythmic lapping of the waves. She is quiet before adding: 'He was going fast. The bike and car burst into flames. When I reached him, I pulled him from the burning wreckage but his body . . .' Her voice fades into a long silence.

She turns to me and asks: 'Are you sure you want to know?'
'Yes, if you want to tell me.'

Ingrid picks up a pebble and studies it before continuing. 'He lay in my arms, he was still alive.' She breathes heavily, her voice small, barely audible. 'I screamed. Someone pulled me from him, then more people came and took me away.' I turn to look at her. Tears slide down her cheeks, leaving wet streaks, and she takes another deep breath. 'It was awful. You cannot imagine.'

As if suddenly physically exhausted, she rests her forehead in the palm of one hand. She leans forward, studying the pebble, and remains like that for some time, before looking out over the dark expanse of lake. 'I just wanted to be with him. I knew . . . Somehow, I knew, it was all finished. One minute we had our future in front of us, full of life, and the next moment it was all gone . . . It happened so quickly. People were holding me back. I became calm, so they would let go of me and I could hold him. A doctor was there soon.' She speaks in a monotone and closes her fingers around the smooth stone. 'They let me hold my husband's hands. I could see his legs were broken, as if they did not belong to him. I couldn't look at his body. I squeezed his hand and asked him if he could hear me. I looked at his face and felt him squeeze my hand back. I told him I loved him and he pressed my hand again, three times. "*Ich liebe dich.*" I love you.' Her fist clenches the stone three times as she speaks, the veins on the back of her hand dilating. 'He always did that.'

She opens the palm of her hand, the pebble a pool of darkness against the paleness of her skin. 'His eyes couldn't focus. He was staring straight ahead, empty. He couldn't see me any more, but he could still hear me. Blood was coming out of his mouth, nose, ears. He was dying. The doctor told me he would be OK, but I knew. He was letting himself go; he wasn't fighting, his hand was no longer pressing mine. A helicopter arrived from the hospital and then fire trucks and ambulances.'

She is silent a long time. 'His leather suit was burnt.' She inhales deeply. 'It had a strong smell.' She breathes out, then in deeply again and holds her breath. I sit there equally still, not sure what to do or say. Not even the morepork cries now. 'It's cold,' she says finally, with a shiver, letting the air out of her lungs. But she does not get up.

'After a month I needed to get back to work, to keep my mind occupied, otherwise I would go crazy. The children helped but when the school year ended, I wanted to go away. The headmaster told me to take as much time as I needed; the job would always be waiting. My husband had been dead for almost a year and yet I felt as if he were looking over my shoulder all the time. It was so real, I could feel him beside me, hear his words. Sometimes I would conclude unfinished conversations with him; I could imagine him whispering to me, as if he was physically there, but had suddenly become invisible.' She is quiet some time before she says: 'I decided to come here to New Zealand. The night before I left Germany, I had a dream about him. He said he couldn't follow me if I went so far away. He wasn't angry in my dream, he was letting go, letting me let go of him. I was sad, but happy somehow that he couldn't follow me, as if I could begin life again, and begin to forget.' She adds, as if reciting a memorised line, 'It is better that I forget and smile now, than remember and be sad forever. He will always be with me anyway.'

She grips the pebble tightly, reaches back and throws it so far into the murkiness of the lake that we neither see nor hear the splash.

The words of a popular love song permeate my subconscious. I am unsure of where I am, my eyes are still closed. I open my eyes. In a bunk next to me, Ingrid is burrowed into her sleeping-bag. A radio alarm clock in the kitchen has been set for six in the morning and tuned to the local radio station by a previous tramper. The plaintive song penetrates the silence of the bunkhouse. I listen to the end of the song before sliding out of the sleeping-bag, wrapping it around me. I boil water for tea and offer Ingrid a cup as she lies in bed, still bundled in her sleeping-bag. My breath is visible in the cold air.

'I couldn't sleep,' she says, reaching out for the mug. 'It was freezing during the night.'

We converse over several cups of tea, and this time I do much of the talking, opening up to myself as much as to her. I do not hold back. It is almost nine when I start to pack, almost too late to catch the scheduled water taxi to the starting point of the Waikaremoana Track.

'Why don't you join me?' I ask, knowing Ingrid has just completed the four-day walk. For the first time on this trip I have met someone I want to tramp with.

'Do it again?' Laughing, she rolls onto her stomach, sips the tea and contemplates the idea? 'Yes, why not?' she says finally. 'I would like to, I like your company.'

'I like your company too.'

She gets out of her sleeping-bag and packs in a rush. 'I don't have much food, just lentils and bean sprouts.'

'I have lots of fresh fruit and vegetables, enough for two.' And no split peas. 'Don't worry about it.'

The only passengers, we catch the water taxi across the lake to Onepoto, and begin the long climb up Panekiri Bluff. The track leads through the Armed Constabulary Redoubt, where Te Kooti, the Maori religious leader, retreated after escaping from Chatham Island and making a series of raids on East Cape. He hid in these forests, successfully evading British troops. They never caught him and eventually he was formally pardoned. Ingrid and I walk without talking, one behind the other, through the mysterious and dense rainforest. It is easy to see how Te Kooti hid here so effectively.

Occasionally the path skirts the edge of the bluff, providing a panoramic view of the shoreline of the lake around which we will walk. Near the top of the cliffs we stop to picnic, our feet hanging over a perpendicular drop. The clouds are dark and low but occasionally great shafts of sunlight break through the gaps, suddenly illuminating the sad battleship-grey waters with sparkling pools of quicksilver.

Ingrid says: 'There are supposed to be wild cattle here.'

'Which, like all introduced non-farm animals, are fair game for shooting,' I remark. In my peripheral vision I see a man's head pop up over the bushes. His face is flushed and dominated by a huge walrus moustache. Although slightly thinning on top, he has long, blond-grey hair which falls loosely over his bulky shoulders. He has sympathetic features and a dimpled smile so big his twinkling eyes almost disappear. When he sees I have noticed him, he nods affably. 'Hello!' I call out.

'Hi!' he replies diffidently. Despite his considerable height and size, he speaks softly. He resembles a large but timid mythical creature of the rainforest.

I have some fresh fruit and vegies in the pack: apples, oranges, apricots and carrots. I grab an apple and lob it to him; he catches it effortlessly and munches contently from the safety of the bushes.

I try to include him in our impromptu picnic. 'Where are you from?' I enquire.

'New Hampshire.'

'How long are you here for?' Ingrid does not turn around.

'Some months, just getting away from home for the winter.' He remains partially hidden by the bushes, seemingly too shy to emerge from the woods.

I hesitate to approach; I do not want to scare him away. 'What's your name?' I ask encouragingly.

'Pat.' He turns slightly and I notice his green US army backpack.

'I'm Andrew, this is Ingrid.' I throw him another apple, slightly to one side of him. Ingrid turns to look, smiles, but does not say anything.

Pat steps out from behind the bushes to catch the fruit, leaning on a stiff pole, his walking stick. Ingrid and I repack our bags and continue walking, encouraging Pat to join us by engaging him in conversation and handing him a constant supply of fresh fruit, which he accepts gratefully.

Near the top of the bluffs, we meet a middle-aged woman sitting alone on wooden steps which lead up a steep rock face. She wears a green shirt and green fleece jacket, and looks like a retired teacher. 'Are you the hut warden?' I ask.

'No, but I wish I was.'

'What do you mean?'

'I've been walking this route around the lake for three days and every night there has been a group of students with two teachers. The kids are totally out of control. DOC has already expelled eleven of them from the park for smoking marijuana and stealing chicken eggs left as baits in possum traps. There's still twenty-eight of them left and they're staying at Panekiri Hut, just up there.' She points above us. 'It's so noisy and chaotic that I came down here to get some peace and quiet. Screaming kids, sixteen-year-olds with hormones working overtime. At night, the testosterone levels are palpable.'

'You could pretend you're DOC with that green coordinated outfit you're wearing,' I suggest.

'They know I'm not DOC. But you could pretend' – her face brightens as she studies me – 'with that huge green backpack.' She looks at Ingrid and Pat. 'The three of you look exactly like DOC workers. You could scare them and get them to behave.' She smiles at the thought.

'Should we?' I ask Pat and Ingrid. A mischievous glint in Ingrid's eyes indicates yes. Pat smiles in tacit agreement. I admonish, 'No laughing, OK? We don't want to give the game away.'

We walk to the hut, some fifteen minutes up the path. Outside, two elderly couples lie on the grass, apparently displaced by the rambunctious kids. Boots and scraps of clothing lie scattered about.

The hut is in a state of total chaos. Dirty pots and pans clutter the room. There is so much food everywhere, it looks as if they have had a food fight.

I bark: 'Who's in charge here?'

Pat blocks the door in his military-style boots, legs astride, his walking stick in the crook of his arm like an assault rifle nestled against his barrel chest. There is a stunned silence.

Finally, one of the students answers: 'One teacher's asleep and the other is outside somewhere.'

The teacher comes out of the bunkroom, apparently woken by our presence. 'Are these your students?' I snap at him authoritatively.

'Yes.'

'Looks like things are out of control here,' I remark, trying to increase the bass in my voice and puffing out my chest like a pigeon.

He looks around guiltily. 'I wouldn't say they're out of control exactly . . .' The students listen, frozen in place. 'If you are staying, we can find some empty bunks . . .' he says apprehensively.

Pat looks around, and as he marches into the centre of the room, he booms, 'We're the special anti-drug SWAT Team. Been flown by helicopter from Washington to keep an eye on what's going on here. We'll be sleeping in the bush tonight' – he indicates with a toss of his head. 'Just to make sure things don't get out of hand again.' He has a natural authority and were I not in on the hoax, I would believe him myself. The two elderly couples, who have now been joined by the woman who put us up to this, stand in the doorway. He says to them sternly, so the kids can hear: 'If you have any problems with things in here during the night, let us know. We'll be right out there in case you need us.' He points with his square jaw at the bush outside. 'Any of you still got drugs?'

There is a unanimous shaking of heads.

The five adults smile and say: 'Thanks.' The teacher shifts uncomfortably, not quite sure what to make of all this, but probably happy to go along with the Forces of Good that have suddenly shown up on the doorstep. The students sit stunned, eyes wide. Just goes to show the extent of global integration and brainwashing when a SWAT Team is plausibly sent out from Washington to take care of some misbehaving Kiwi kids. You can see some of them thinking: 'A SWAT team from Washington? Cool!' Pat and Ingrid are pretty convincing in their roles. Maybe I look pretty kuh-ool in their company too.

I turn to Pat, trying not to smile, putting him on the spot: 'Tell them what we do with students we catch messing around with possum bait.' I wouldn't know how to swat a fly, never mind take out a terrorist group or a class of grass-smoking kids on a school outing.

Pat does not hesitate to reply: 'We stake 'em to the ground, smother them in peanut butter and let the possums at 'em.' Two boys are nervously fumbling with something in their hands. He points his stick accusingly at them. 'What have you got there?'

'Tea bags.'

'That better not be dope.'

'The ones with the dope have been taken away.'

'You better be right, otherwise you're in deep shit, and not the good shit you might want to be in either.'

'Yes.'

With that, the three of us stride off towards the next hut, giggling. When we arrive at Waiopaoa Hut, we hoist our packs onto three-tiered bunks. Ingrid and I go down to the lake to swim. When we return, it seems Pat has gone missing. I ask Ingrid. 'Where's Pat?'

'Here,' Pat replies. He has taken a bunk in the top corner with barely enough headroom to tuck his body under the roof, despite the fact that we have the hut to ourselves and there are plenty of bunks with easier access. He has concealed himself, his army pack and his walking stick, as if he were hiding in a bunker from the Viet Cong.

'Aren't you eating?' I ask.

'Already ate.'

While cleaning my teeth after breakfast, I read a sign warning of the dangers of living in New Zealand:

Safety
In the case of earthquakes, move to higher ground and keep away from large trees, which may shed branches. You need to be at least five metres above lake level and to stay there at least fifteen minutes after the last shock.

The worst part of the day is in the morning, peeling off clothes still warm from sleeping in them and putting on cold clothes, still damp and sweaty from the previous day. Our clothes smell musty, like a wet haystack, a strong earthy odour that is not unpleasant.

The morning looms overcast and cold. We tramp clockwise around the lake, crossing a small stream with a suspended bridge made from chain-link fence and wooden flooring. Beside it is a massive bridge under construction, big enough for trucks. On the path we meet an elderly Kiwi couple who have come across the lake in their motor boat.

'Did you see the bridge?' the wife asks. We could not have missed it. 'It'll compete with the Auckland Harbour Bridge by the time they've finished it. Ever since the Cave Creek disaster, where fourteen people died on a collapsed viewing platform, DOC has been paranoid about construction, but this is ridiculous. Every plank of wood crossing a trickle of water has an orange tag on it, with a serial number.'

Ingrid moves ahead and Pat brings up the rear. While crossing a small stream almost overgrown with toitoi grass and ferns, I stop to admire the view. Pat waits patiently on the other side, leaning on his walking stick, half disguised in the tall grass. We conduct a verbal volleyball game across the gap, discussing women, marriage, children, the meaning of life. Then Ingrid reappears, interrupting us.

'Are you OK?' she asks, beads of sweat dripping off her face.

'Sure, why?'

'I waited for you for so long I thought maybe one of you was injured.'

I laugh.

'Why are you laughing?' she asks, looking aggrieved.

'I've been walking alone for months. In that time anything could have happened to me and I wouldn't have been missed for ages. Now I stop to talk for a few minutes, on this easy track and you come searching for me.'

'A few minutes? I was waiting an hour.' She is not so much annoyed as genuinely concerned.

I hug her, and say, 'Ingrid, it's a nice feeling having someone keep a look out for me.'

We continue walking and half an hour later are standing on the lip of a cup-like depression, overlooking waterfalls. At the bottom is a tumble of smooth rocks and a deep clear pool, surrounded by ferns and shadowed by tall beech and rimu trees festooned with bearded moss. The sun pokes out from behind thick, puffy clouds and illuminates the delicate lace-work of falling water. When the clouds cover the sun again, it is as if the lights have been dimmed on a stage. We gaze intently, mesmerised by the light and water show.

'It doesn't get more beautiful than this anywhere,' Pat comments. 'Anywhere I've been anyway.'

Ingrid climbs down to the pool to cool off.

I ask him: 'Backpacked around Asia much?'

He laughs ironically. 'Sure, but it was more terrorism than tourism.'

'You mean in Vietnam?'

He replies, diffidently: 'I was in a special long-range reconnaissance team up the border areas.' He stares ahead and I try to imagine him walking around the jungle, waiting to be ambushed. Despite the thinning grey hair, it is not hard to imagine him twenty-five years younger, lean and hard, confident with the ignorance of youth.

'We were parachuted in, worked in teams of two, sometimes for weeks at a time before they bailed us out with a chopper dust off.' He is reflective for some time. 'Now I see tourists wearing T-shirts with: "I was on such-and-such adventure tour in Vietnam." ' He speaks quietly, staring at the waterfalls. 'Still can't cope with it; not because I've got anything against the Vietnamese, but just because . . . it seems such a colossal waste of lives and effort when, not so long after the Vietnam war, young Americans who never had to deal with the fighting are going there on adventure holidays.' His eyes blink thoughtfully with memories he keeps to himself. 'Guess I was on an adventure tour there myself,' he concludes finally, with a shake of his head. 'We were fighting the spread of Communism; now American companies support Communist China's economic growth. If I had to do it again, I'd be a conscientious objector.'

He rests his chin on his stick for a while before he stands upright again. 'The real irony is, I'd be a defector knowing what I do now. That says something, because we were sent in to locate defectors so that they could be assassinated by a follow-up team.' He is so quiet, I can hear him breathing. 'Then, I believed in what we were doing. We were given the choice after that, either to extend our tour of duty by some months, and when we got back to the States be discharged immediately, or to leave Vietnam on schedule, but spend more time back in the States, but still in the army. I extended my tour in Vietnam. Within days of getting back to the States, I was no longer in the military and wandering around city streets. I thought everyone had changed while I was away. Only later I realised all my friends were still the same, it was me who had changed.'

He studies the falls, the forest and the idyllic pool below us. Ingrid climbs out of the water and sits beside it, contemplating. 'I wish we had been sent here to the rainforests of New Zealand, instead of back home to the States. After Vietnam, we needed to adjust. Get a chance to walk around in this kind of bush, without worrying about being shot at. Without worrying about anything. Would have been good therapy.'

Ingrid climbs back into the pool. I feel like joining her but do not want to interrupt Pat. I am about to say something, thinking he has stopped, but then he adds: 'After Vietnam I went to college. Got a Bachelor of Arts degree in English Literature. Took a course on women's issues.' He laughs. 'The first day I walked into the class, they thought I had come into the wrong room. They were all women. I told them I was a lesbian in disguise.' He shrugs. 'At college I had summer jobs in construction work. My dad got me the job, he was a construction worker, as was his dad. I finished my degree and now I'm still a construction worker. Sometimes I feel like I'm paving the world one square metre at a time.'

He shakes his head. 'This is my seventh trip to New Zealand. It's all I save up for. Just walking around the bush for a few months at a time, remembering and trying to forget the war. I had nightmares for years. I saw bad things in Vietnam I hope never to see in my life again. I experienced and did bad things myself. It's a rehabilitation process for me, walking in this jungle. I'm still working at it.' He laughs self-consciously before continuing. It hardly seems possible this gentle giant could ever have done anything bad. 'When I first went out to Vietnam, I thought I was immortal. That soon changed. If you've any kind of imagination, you're convinced you're gonna die. I felt intensely alive in Vietnam because I was so aware of being mortal, as opposed to being shot at and killed. In New Zealand I have the same feeling. Walking in the bush here, I feel alive again; but this time it is no longer conditional on surviving the day.'

Ingrid sits on the edge of the rocks, watching the water falling into the pool. Pat asks, 'How long have you and Ingrid known each other?'

'Met her the evening before we met you.'

He steps back. 'You're kidding. I thought you were friends from way back.'

'Just seems that way,' I reply, as Ingrid climbs back up to join us. 'We did a lot of talking that first night. Didn't hold anything back.'

We walk in silence after that, Ingrid leading, Pat following. By the time we arrive at the next hut, it is already early evening. There is no one else there. Ingrid lights a candle she has brought with her and I start preparing dinner. Pat pulls out a zip-lock bag with ready-made peanut butter and jam sandwiches inside. The jam is bleeding into the bread like beetroot juice. He consumes pre-packed sandwiches for breakfast, lunch and dinner. They hardly seem an adequate meal for a man of Pat's size.

'Are you sure you've got enough to eat?' Ingrid asks. Last night he had insisted his sandwiches were all he wanted or needed, but we have been walking for two days now.

'You'll starve,' I say.

Pat glances over at the pot of spaghetti that Ingrid and I share between us. 'I'm trying to lose a bit of weight,' he says, taking a big bite out of a small sandwich. He is thickset, maybe a little chubby around the belly, but certainly not fat.

Ingrid and I could easily polish off the spaghetti, but we offer to share it with Pat. 'Come on, we'd never be able to finish it.'

He declines at first: 'No thanks.'

Finally we get him to accept and he eagerly devours the pasta. Satiated, he leans back happily against the wooden wall of the hut. Now in an expansive mood, he tells us: 'I remember being invited to a Kiwi family's house for dinner on my first trip to New Zealand. They heaped so much meat on my plate and after the first helping they asked me if I wanted more. I couldn't, and replied: "No thanks, I'm stuffed." There was an awful silence around the table. Someone started chuckling. I didn't know what I'd said wrong. "No, really, I'm stuffed," I repeated. Then someone burst out laughing and they explained that "being stuffed" wasn't exactly the right thing to say after being invited over for a meal. Means you're buggered or something like that.'

It is misty and drizzly outside. A breeze blows ripples on the rocky shore. For the second morning in a row, Pat is wandering around the forest somewhere, having already slipped out of his bunk before dawn so silently and stealthily that neither Ingrid nor I heard him leave. There is a loneliness and sadness about Pat, the ultimate Lonely Guy looking for himself, looking for the youth he lost in Vietnam, looking for something, although much the same can be said of Ingrid and myself.

Ingrid lights a fire in the pot-bellied stove. The wet wood takes time to catch and smoke billows from the chimney. Pat emerges from the mist. He is clean-shaven and his grey walrus moustache is perfectly groomed. He opens another zip-lock plastic bag with more leaking peanut butter and jam sandwiches inside. After breakfast, we diligently clean out the hut so it is considerably tidier than when we arrived, and head into the dense forest towards Te Puna Hut, arriving there by mid-afternoon.

We can smell the bacon, sausages, beans and French fries before we enter the hut. A butcher shop worth of red steaks and sausages is in a couple of open coolers, a plastic garbage bag is stuffed with empty beer bottles and several full bottles of Scotch sit on a counter. Pat can scarcely believe his eyes when he sees the food, the idea of surviving on peanut butter and jam sandwiches for three days on the basis of losing weight finally having worn thin, even if he has not. He hovers around the unprotected food like a hungry black bear, as if just being near it would replenish him. Three men in shorts and gumboots ignore us, behaving almost as if we had intruded on their private bach, their own cabin. Finishing breakfast, they leave the remaining tucker in the closed chilly bin, but pack their motor boat with beer and whisky.

It rains again but inside it feels warm and cosy. When it gets dark we make dinner together and talk for hours. Ingrid plays with the flickering candle, recycling the dripping wax to make it last longer. The scene is timeless, like a replica of an old oil painting, with shadows cast by the warm candlelight, the play of subdued colours tinged by an eerie, orange glow.

We are in our bunks fast asleep when the fishermen return. I awaken when I hear the outboard engine and the scrunch of the aluminium hull as it scrapes on the stony beach, followed by the voices of the men as they clamber out. Judging by their loud conversation and their clumsiness when they enter the hut, they are drunk. We hear them noisily preparing dinner although it is well past midnight and it is clear that they keep drinking and get progressively more intoxicated. An argument breaks out; one insists on water skiing but the owner of the motor boat refuses and they shove each other around. One leaves to start the boat but we hear him stumble off the porch steps and fall, apparently passing out. Eventually the other two climb into their bunks on the other side of the hut. I look at my watch; it is four in the morning.

Next morning the fishermen are either fast asleep or passed out, two in the bunks, one sprawled outside beside the path. None of them stirs when we leave. They were probably so drunk they won't remember the acrimonious session last night and continue the best of friends, as if nothing had happened.

When we arrive at the dock where the water taxi will pick us up, Pat decides to stay, to haunt Lake Waikaremoana for another couple of days. Ingrid and I get into the boat and wave back at Pat. He is half-hidden in the bushes, just as he was when we first met him. Leaving him behind, there is a sense of losing a close friend.

The gregarious water-taxi operator asks us: 'So where you heading?'

Ingrid says: 'Back to the South Island.'

I tell him: 'Gisborne and the East Cape.'

He says: 'I'm going there myself, trailing my boat to get it serviced. Come with me if you want.'

The suggestion is unexpected and a bonus. Hitching up East Cape will not be easy because there is so little traffic. I accept his offer, knowing Ingrid must head down to Wellington to catch the ferry, which she has already booked and paid for. If she misses the ferry, it will be difficult reserving another passage at short notice.

The sadness we feel leaving Pat behind is compounded when Ingrid and I reach the bunkhouse, where she packs up her car to head south for the ferry. We exchange addresses, writing in each other's address books; the formal ritual of travellers reluctant to admit the significance of departure, unwilling to concede closure of a friendship just begun. She drives off, waving out of the window as long as I remain in sight; within minutes, I feel lonelier than when I arrived here four days ago.

I shuffle around moodily until the water-taxi operator signals that he is ready to leave. I push my pack over the transom into the back of his boat, which is now sitting high and dry on the trailer, and climb into the front passenger seat of his car.

He is happy to have someone to talk to. 'The local Maori

accused me of taking jobs from them when I started this business,' he tells me almost straightaway. 'There weren't any kayaks or water taxis operating here before, so I'm creating jobs, and not taking them. But none of them wants to work for me. Some of the Maori, not all, say this is their land. I ask them: "Which tribe?" They fought over it so much it wasn't clear whose tribal land it was anyway. Now they want royalties from the Waitangi Tribunal for the hydro stations generating power from the lake. They say it's their lake, their water. I just tell them "their" water disappeared out of the lake a long time ago, and if they can show me which piece of water's "theirs", they can gladly have it back.'

I sit listening to him, my mind not quite focused, still thinking back to the time spent with Ingrid and Pat.

On the coastal road to Gisborne, the old sheep paddocks have been converted to maize and squash fields, vineyards or orchards. My driver points out the landscape: 'All over the East Coast, land that looked like this gave good stocking rates for sheep and cattle. Once the soil's nutrient content was depleted and exposed to the full effects of erosion, without its original tree cover, it became very unstable. Now the depleted hillsides are being replanted with radiata pine. In ten years they will undoubtedly realise they've stuffed up doing that too.'

We drive past a roadside billboard advertising beer: 'If you want me to spend more time in the kitchen, put more beer in the fridge'.

The backpackers lodge in Gisborne is an imposing former convent, built in 1930. I ring the doorbell, feeling dwarfed by the massive wooden front doors. A woman with heavy hips and a flowery skirt opens them. She shows me around the convent, with its high-ceilinged rooms and rimu-wood cupboards, floors and staircases. The lounge is recognisable as the old chapel, with high stained-glass windows and two confessionals built into the wall, but now it is furnished with a pool table and a cinema-sized television.

I ask the manager, as I follow her around: 'What's there to do in Gisborne?'

'Nothing,' she replies.

'Sounds good to me.' No bungee jumping, no jet boating, no jet skis, no rafting, no drunken fishermen. There is so little action here, even the convent closed down for lack of pregnant unmarried teenagers, before being resurrected as a backpackers lodge and rooming house for itinerant vegetable pickers. Gisborne is an authentic New Zealand town and that is enough to enchant me.

I select one of the rooms formerly occupied by nuns. It's my first overnight stay in a convent, and as I lie in bed staring at the high ceiling, I try to imagine what the previous occupants of this bed thought and dreamt every night as they lay here. Were the nuns lonely? Did they miss home? Did they dream of romance?

I console my lonely self with the concept of a nun's lifelong celibacy and devotion to God. Perhaps it is auspicious, lying alone in a nun's bed in a convent. I mean, there could be a dormant hot line from this mattress to heaven just waiting to be reactivated. Lying prone in bed, I press my palms together, close my eyes and cast out a supplication, just in case.

EAST CAPE

The road passes alongside endless stretches of deserted beaches. There are few houses or settlements. An old furniture-removal truck, apparently a holiday home, lies half-buried in the sand dunes, stranded like a shipwreck.

A young sheep shearer gives me a lift to Hicks Bay where I find a backpackers lodge situated on a small cove, with its own beach. The arrival of a German woman interrupts my reading at the kitchen table. She unpacks her food bags. Despite her poor English, I understand that she is a scientist, homoeopath and author.

She explains: 'I use a number of different oils extracted from plants grown in New Zealand, including the manuka bush, or tea-tree. These oils help many of my patients in Germany recover from illnesses that Western medicine has been unable to cure, including cancer and depression. I am here to collect oil extracts from my suppliers and to find new sources, maybe even new oils. And what about you? What are you doing here?'

'Mostly walking in the rainforest for four months,' I reply.

'Is it good?'

'Very good. I feel a tangible sense of wellbeing. I imagine it's as if I'm on some kind of drug.'

She laughs. 'You are. The nose is the hot line to the brain.' She continues, as she selects food for her dinner. 'There is no doubt that there is a psycho-chemical reaction. The fragrances from the forest, including perhaps the manuka bush, the tea-tree, are being absorbed directly by the brain.' She chops garlic. 'It is not surprising you feel so good. That is what my therapy with depressed patients is all about; to absorb the healing properties of the manuka oil and other trees. The only difference is that you are wandering around in the rainforest, going through the aromatherapy in a natural setting, while my patients are in a sterile clinic, doing the same thing, in less harmonious surroundings. You are lucky.'

She scrapes the chopped garlic into a pan. 'It is a good idea doing what you are doing: looking after your soul and body, before something is wrong with it. Preventive medicine and therapy is much more effective than curing. We should all invest the time in a long walk, especially in the rainforests, every year, just as we have life-insurance policies with an annual premium that we must pay. People are too busy making money to worry about their health until it is too late. Then, if they are so fortunate, they come to see me and maybe get a little bit better. If they are not so fortunate, they are ending up in hospital, or maybe they are dead.'

I continue around East Cape and a Maori schoolteacher pulls over at the empty junction off Hicks Bay, to pick me up. She drives slowly and speaks quietly, with deliberation and in a self-effacing manner. In response to my persistent questions, she tells me about her tribe, the Ngati Porou, and the land they were handed back through the Waitangi Tribunal.

'We produce farming and forestry products now. The farm is managed and run by staff under a board of trustees. From the profits, educational grants are given to applicants and seed capital for small businesses. I am proud of the way our trust is run, and what it is doing on behalf of my people. It is managed on business lines and employees are hired through local advertisements. There is no corruption and no favouritism. It's the first of such lands given back to the Maori that has become completely independent.'

The road is winding and narrow, with little traffic either way. She waves at the drivers we pass. The few homes are scattered, isolated, almost hidden in the bush.

'Can you speak Maori?' I ask.

'Yeah, but not very well. I moved up to East Cape from the South Island as an adult. Down in Dunedin, where I grew up, there are more Chinese now than there are Maori. This' – she indicates with a sweep of a hand – 'is originally my home area. My ancestors were forcibly moved away from here to the South Island last century, as punishment because they pulled out the surveying stakes of the pakeha settlers when they took our land.'

Her Maori history is learnt not only from listening to her grandmother, but from extensive reading. 'Heaps of Maori in the North Island can speak Maori. They learn it from their grandparents. My own grandparents were beaten for speaking the Maori language at school, but now my people are learning to speak our own language again.'

I have noticed that the Maori talk of 'my people' as if there were some inherent solidarity to being Maori. I suppose there is, when they are aligned against the pakeha.

'I'm going full on to learn Maori,' she continues. 'When I moved up here, I had distant relatives I had never met, but they accepted me anyway. That is the way it is with Maori. If you are from the same canoe, the same mountain, the same river, then you are treated as family. I can tell you more about the seven different tribes of the great *waka* canoes than I can tell you about the different counties in New Zealand.'

She pulls over to the side of the road to drop me off in front of her school. 'I'd invite you in for a tea, but then I'd be late for my class. If you are still here during my lunchbreak, I'll come and get you and we can have lunch together.'

Although marked on the map, Potaka has only a schoolhouse and nothing else. Must be difficult for touring cyclists planning to buy food, when they get to places marked on their maps only to find nothing there, not even a store. I lean my pack against a fence and wait.

The tops of the monocultured radiata pine-covered hills are hidden in mist. It looks like it is going to rain. To pass the time I stretch, cut my fingernails with the scissors of my Swiss army knife, examine hangnails with the knife's magnifying glass and pull out offending nose hairs with the tweezers, which makes me teary-eyed. Then I put the handy knife away and collect garbage lying beside the road.

A small hatchback pulls up, driven by a young man with a shaved head, earrings and a baseball cap worn backwards. He wears a T-shirt printed with the motto 'Life is short, play hard'. Leaning over, he looks out the open passenger window. 'Where are you going?'

'Anywhere,' I reply. He has a tuft of yellow beard right under his lower lip and nowhere else, as if it were something that is not supposed to be there; like fried egg yoke dribbling down his chin. I want to wipe it off for him.

'Cool.' He says it, kuh-ool, just like the others. 'I'm Scott and I'm cruising around looking for good surf.'

'Crisp,' I reply.

'Crisp?'

'Yeah, means cool, but it's cooler to say "crisp" than it is to say "cool",' I bullshit.

We haul his surfboard out of the car and strap it onto the roof rack so there is room for me in the car. I sit in the passenger seat, holding a dangerously flicking fishing rod away from my face.

'On holiday?' I ask as we pick up momentum on the empty road. This guy should also be on a race track.

He laughs, his eyes hidden by Ninja sunglasses. 'Don't have a job.'

'How do you manage to pay for your surfing?' I turn around to look at the back of the car, stuffed full of food and camping equipment.

'Live cheap in a tent on a beach, smoke dope instead of drinking alcohol; marijuana is everywhere. I live off the dole. Some of my friends even manage to have their names listed twice, so they can collect double the dole. Inefficient system,' he concludes happily.

At Waihu Bay, my laid-back driver stops and removes binoculars from the glove compartment. He examines the surf. 'No good wraps, onshore wind and the waves are just crashing.' The weather is misty and it looks as if it could start raining. We continue driving, and around a bend in the narrow road he slams on the brakes to avoid three horses ambling casually down the middle of the road. When we continue on our way I keep both hands holding onto the dashboard, eyes riveted on the road. The only time we slow down is when we go up steep hills and the small Japanese engine struggles with the load. Going down hills, it's as if his big toe is glued to the accelerator pedal, which in turn is welded to the floorboards. At Raukokore, where he thankfully stops yet again in his serious but esoteric examination of the surf, I explore a wooden church. The church, built on the wind-swept peninsula in 1894, has a hand-written note tacked to the front door: 'Please excuse the fishy smell. We have a family of penguins nesting right under the floor by the door. Mother penguin is very busy bringing in fish to feed the *whanau*.'

We continue, whizzing past an ornately carved *marae* building in a school ground. Scott tells me: 'Some of my best friends are Maori but I resent the fact that they get scholarships to go to universities, overseas or here. At school, OK they were clever, but they were lazy as could be too, and now they're getting scholarships and grants from the Maori trusts.' He hands me a bag of crisps and takes a corner at excessive speed, one hand on the steering wheel. The car rolls alarmingly and I keep both hands on the dashboard, in case we meet another posse of horses straddling the centreline. Released from my clutches, the fishing rod flicks continuously in my face.

Scott continues: 'I also resent the fact that 90 per cent of prisoners in jail are Maori. It angers me when land is given back to the Maori and they sell it to Koreans or Japs who exploit it to make money, and not necessarily in the best interests of New Zealanders.' He takes off his baseball cap to scratch his bald scalp. 'Maori are great people. My best mates are Maori. But just a few bad ones are spoiling it for the others. If I were prime minister, I would give the foreigners five years to sell the land back to New Zealanders. As a Kiwi I would be willing to accept a lower standard of living to pay for that, just so we can have our land and keep New Zealand the way it is, rather than sell it all and have no land in the future.'

He stops to examine the surf at yet another beach. I sit patiently as he studies the wave action. It starts to rain, and despite the slippery road we cruise through the landscape as fast as before. He launches into the Maori issue with renewed vigour.

'When we play rugby, we do the *haka* as a challenge to the opposing team. Right?' He studies me expectantly.

'Right,' I reply, keeping my eyes on the road.

'OK, look at New Zealand's national All Blacks rugby team. They are mixed pakeha and Maori. However, the Maoris have their own Maori team, with no whites in it. That's racist. There's no all-white rugby team. They'd never allow an all-white rugby team. But an all-Maori rugby team? That's OK. They want it all their way, there's no give and take.'

I sit there quietly. He has been generous enough to give me a lift and besides, if I start challenging him, he is likely to throw me out.

Perhaps he takes my silence as tacit approval of his opinions.

'Another thing that gets up my nose is this stuff about the Maori being conservationists. In prehistoric New Zealand, there were flightless birds called the moa. There were eleven species, some not much bigger than geese and others that were giants weighing three times as much as that horse out there.' He points at a scraggly horse in a paddock, its lower lip hanging loose from its mouth, a lazy back leg cocked. 'The biggest moa were the tallest birds that ever lived. They survived changes in climate and vegetation brought about by ice ages and volcanic eruptions, but the Maori exterminated the moa in a few hundred years. So don't tell me Maori are conservationists.'

Rolling about on the dashboard is a paperback, *A Good Keen Man* by Barry Crump. To keep it from sliding about I pick it up and flip through the pages. Mr Crump, a hunter of some repute according to his autobiography, details how many deer he slaughtered over a period of years.

Scott tells me: 'That's New Zealand's best selling book.'

Either that or biographies of twenty-year-old rugby players, I think to myself.

'With all the land claims made by the Maori, who do you think will benefit?' Scott asks me, rhetorically. 'Not the average Maori, I can tell you. Just the lawyers and accountants. They're ripping off their own people. And these Maori businesses they set up with the trust funds? They go bankrupt. Why shouldn't they? The Maori haven't worked for it. It's just a heap of money or land thrown at them. They have no experience handling it. When they go bankrupt owing money, the land they own is untouchable. When it happens to my dad, who is a farmer, he loses everything, including his land.' He shakes his head. 'Seems our political leaders are a few thrusts short of an orgasm to be handing all this land back to the Maori.'

'Few thrusts short of an orgasm? What's that mean?'

'Means they're a couple of sandwiches short of a picnic; a tinnie short of a six-pack; a couple of *kumara* short of a *hangi*.'

New Zealanders have made considerable efforts to redress wrongs perpetrated against the indigenous people of the country they colonised. They have certainly gone to greater lengths and had greater success than the Australians or Americans. Kiwis have something to be proud of in this respect. As a non-New Zealander, it strikes me as a shame that some Kiwis, like Scott, do not appreciate the extent to which their identity is tied to their Maori heritage.

Lightning flashes and thunder rumbles in the distance, as rain inundates the car. One aspect of hitchhiking is you get to meet all sorts. It is dry and warm in the car; it is pouring with rain outside, and cold. Pragmatism prevails and I keep my opinions to myself.

COROMANDEL PENINSULA

It is Waitangi Day, a national public holiday previously known as New Zealand Day. I read the caption under a photograph on the front page of the newspaper: 'The most serious incident at the celebrations of the Treaty of Waitangi involved protesters scaling the flag pole, removing the New Zealand flag, the Union Jack and the Navy ensign, and hoisting flags representing Maori sovereignty'.

Inside is a piece:

LET'S RETURN TO WAITANGI, SAYS GOVERNOR-GENERAL
The Governor-General, Sir Michael Hardie Boys, wants to see the Waitangi Day celebrations return to Waitangi, 'the traditional and proper place' to celebrate the signing of the treaty. Speaking yesterday at a function at Government House, he said the Wellington location was 'remote from historical settings'. The official commemorations were transferred to Wellington after diplomats and the then Governor-General, Dame Catherine Tizard, were spat at and abused by protesters at Waitangi in 1995. Many New Zealanders saw the treaty as 'an ancient paper of no current relevance', said Sir Michael. But he said justice demanded that the 'genuine wrongs' of the past be redressed because their legacy remained, with Maori comprising 'a substantially disproportionate number of our under-privileged'.

I head to the nearest backpackers lodge in Coromandel Township, passing a bank with muddy gumboots lined up outside and bare-foot farmers inside. In the lounge at the backpackers I sit with a cup of tea and read the visitor's book. In it someone has written:

> The TV thing. Part of the backpacker experience is meeting so many different people and exchanging ideas, experiences, making connections, and all that. As soon as you put that little monster in the room, all this goes out the window. People become alpha zombies, interaction stops.

That evening I ignore the little TV monster and the depressing sight of backpackers in a far-off country hypnotised by American sitcoms. It's sad enough seeing young people letting the lives get sucked out of them at home, but it's even more tragic when they travel the world to vegetate in front of a TV showing familiar sitcoms. I sit alone outside. It is a cool, breezy evening, dominated by a layered sky, cobalt, mauve, purple pastels merging into one another like the washed-out hues of a watercolour painting. These delicate shades are mirrored in a mercurial sea, which is cut symmetrically by long lines of farmed mussel stands. Ponga palms, silhouetted against an orange horizon, frame a sliver of moon floating above the dark hills.

At the northern tip of the Coromandel Peninsula, I stare up at vertical pinnacle rocks and watch formations of gannets glide by. They hitchhike effortlessly on unseen currents of wind, their wings rigid as kites. Lying prone and horizontal on the rocks, my perspective of an overhead puff of cloud drifting by gives the optical illusion that the rock cliff is falling on top of me, as if the clouds were stationary. I sit up to regain a sense of perspective and notice beyond the rocks a pod of dolphins swimming by the headland. First in pairs, then in larger groups, the procession passes by, moving with the wind and the waves. Hundreds, perhaps even a thousand, glistening, smooth backs break the surface of the water in a long line over a kilometre long. I guess these are bottlenose dolphins by their size and shape. They swim past the pinnacle rocks to the calmer waters on the lee side, only a couple of hundred metres offshore, where they appear to be in a holding pattern, perhaps waiting for the others.

Spurred on by Ingrid's stories of swimming with dolphins, I run along the rocks as close as I can get to the dolphins before stripping naked and diving into the water. The ocean is cold. I reach the first dolphins and start singing underwater, with a loud, high-pitched voice. Three dolphins approach me. They are considerably bigger than the duskies. Although their shapes are visible, without goggles they are indistinct, and intimidating as they circle me. The water is chilly and saps my energy. Sensing also that I am being tugged out to sea, I swim against the current sucking me away from shore. There is not much out there to stop me drifting away to the Americas. The rip is strong and faster than I can swim against and I realise with a rising sense of panic that I am being swept out to sea.

My mind grapples with the fact that if I drown, I will have the added ignominy of being plucked out of the frigid water naked. If anyone finds me, that is. I change direction and rather than swim directly against the current, swim obliquely towards shore. Using the swell of the ocean, I coordinate my assault on land with an incoming wave and pull myself up onto the seaweed-covered rocks. Exhausted, I sprawl on the slimy boulders examining scrapes on my knees and shins, which begin to bleed. A little in shock at how close I came to being sucked out to sea, I watch the dolphins jumping out of the water, falling with a splash onto their sides. Hundreds more swim past the tip of the peninsula. When I recover my breath, I walk back on tender bare feet to retrieve my clothes and sandals, exhausted from the exertion of swimming against the current in the cold water.

In the evening, dressed warmly and sitting safely on a rock at the top of a hill, I listen to the breeze. The horizon out at sea is a slightly convex razor edge, broken by Great Barrier Island, Little

Barrier Island and, far to the north, other islands. The sharp evening light reminds me of the light in southern Africa, except that there is no sense of danger. Here, no predators lurk menacingly in the bush, unless you count seventy million possums munching through thousands of tons of greens every night.

The pasture below me is green and very pretty, grazed to resemble a manicured golf course by sheep and cows. But what was it like when this same hillside was covered in kauri forest? Magnificent trees, thousands of years old, cut down so grass can grow to feed domestic animals.

When it gets cold, I retreat down to the hut and notice for the first time a newspaper clipping thumb-tacked to the inside of the front door, obviously placed there as a warning. It is about a fisherman who slipped off the rocks here. He was swept away in the current and never seen again.

COROMANDEL – AUCKLAND – KERIKERI

So many immigrants wanted their quarter-acre section of the 'Promised Land' that it seems to take hours bypassing Auckland's suburban sprawl on the way north. I disembark at the Bay of Islands, where the initial contact between white settlers and the Maori was most intense, and where the Waitangi Treaty was signed. Adjacent tourist-ridden Paihia has 1500-horsepower cigar-shaped motor boats, whisking Japanese visitors on a tight schedule through the marine national park. The rooster tails behind these marine rockets, their almighty roar and the town's prefabricated waterfront motels persuade me to hitchhike further, to a farm hostel just outside Kerikeri.

Claes, a Swede, welcomes me into his beautiful home. He reminds me of one of Santa's helpers, with his pale complexion, white hair and half-moon reading glasses.

The TV news depicts a massacre near National Park, where a man had shot several friends and relatives in a bloody rampage.

191

Claes says: 'Violence comes from America: it's exported through TV, videos, films.'

'That's why we left the United States,' adds his wife, who is American. 'I met Claes when he was in Florida working as a shipwright.' He is some twenty years older than her.

'The whole value system is screwed up there,' Claes continues. 'If you have money, you are made, and everyone looks up to you. In America, they reward material success. If you are not successful, you are nothing. The rich get richer, the poor get poorer. Family values are disappearing.'

'Isn't it getting that way here?' I ask. New Zealand used to have a socialised economy, which has changed in recent years to a user-pays system. 'Hasn't New Zealand's egalitarian society changed to a meritocracy where the rich get richer and the poor get poorer?'

I hit a sore spot with that comment. He nods. 'New Zealand no longer seems so different from the capitalist world of North America.'

'You weren't tempted to go back to Sweden?' I ask. If he wants a welfare state, he could always go home to his native country.

'Sweden?' He shakes his head. 'The grey society. It's OK in the summertime, but in September the skies turn grey, they put on grey suits, wear grey expressions and rush about from job to home, home to job.'

His wife joins in again: 'At school in Florida, our kids had to go through metal detectors, so that the teachers could take knives and guns off eleven-year-olds. That's why we left the US, for our children's sake. It's a lot safer here. But now I feel so cut off, so far away from home.' She becomes emotional, as she thinks about her family.

I understand the feeling. Sometimes it seems that the more choices you have, the more difficult it becomes to find a place to call home.

Claes adds: 'Now it's not so easy any more for our friends to come and visit us.' He pushes the reading glasses up his nose.

'But we like it here.' He glances at his wife, who is wiping a tear from her cheek, then puts his arm comfortingly around her shoulder. 'There's a lot of good things about New Zealand. The climate is nicer than Florida. It's not so hot here.' He is determined to put a positive spin on their move.

I discreetly leave them to sort out their emotions, and explore the farm. At the end of the apple orchard my explorations are impeded by an electric fence. I gingerly touch the bright orange tape with the tip of my finger, to confirm whether the current is switched on or off. No shock, no current. I straddle the fence to get a closer look at some gum trees on the other side and am astride the flimsy barrier when thousands of volts zap my family jewels. I scream in genuine agony. This is a pulse electric fence; testing it quickly with my fingers I had been lucky and missed the shock, but in straddling it for a little longer, I had pushed my luck. I stand there immobilised, as if important parts of me have fused to the fence. I detect a burning odour, and then get zapped again. Defying the forces of gravity, I catapult off the ground and clear the electrified wire before I get seared good and proper.

I limp back to the farmhouse. A backpacker sits on the porch watching me. She has long, fair hair pulled back in a ponytail, clear of her freckled face, and wire-rim spectacles, which give her a bookish appearance.

'Are you OK?' she asks.

'Just a minor discomfort,' I reply, nonchalantly. I climb the steps to the porch, faking a smile. Standing in front of her, I am decidedly bow-legged, as if I had just ridden a horse for a week.

'Are you sure?' she asks again.

'Why, are you a doctor?'

'No, a marine-biology student. I am doing my PhD.' She studies me carefully. 'Are you certain you are all right? You look awful.'

'No, no, I'll be fine.' My voice sounds strange.

'My name is Lisa.'

'From Holland?'

'How did you know?'

'I'm good at detecting accents.' I reach out my hand, still not fully recovered. 'My name is Andrew.'

'English?'

'Born in Canada,' I reply, lowering myself tenderly on a hammock. I still feel nauseous and shift my weight, discreetly spreading my legs apart until I can get reasonably comfortable. Still feeling faint, I brush the top of my head with a hand to see if my hair is standing on end.

'And you are travelling around New Zealand?' I ask. My mind is not as sharp as it was a few minutes ago.

'I'm taking four months off from my studies.' She has a disarming way of staring at me intently.

'Have you had dinner?' I ask, thinking the queasiness in my stomach might be fixed by eating. The hammock sways, just fractionally, but in my current state I am likely to vomit if I continue lying in it. Amazing how sensitive testicles can be. 'I can make us both dinner if you want, it's just as easy as making it for myself.'

Cooking as a team, we wade through the preliminary backpackers' conversation: How long have you been here? Where have you been? Where are you going? Lisa has been all over New Zealand these last four months and she is leaving on the same day as I am. Like me, she started in the south and worked her way north.

We have the farmhouse to ourselves. Claes is out in the fields setting green branches on fire, which is what I had smelled burning; his wife has gone to pick up their two kids from a friend's house.

'What was your most memorable experience here?' I ask.

'The best part of New Zealand for me was the Catlins, in the South Island. I was standing on the beach one evening. It was pouring with rain and the wind was blowing so hard from the sea. I stood there for a long time, feeling it all. There was no one else there. I danced in the rain naked, feeling the drops pelting my body. It was a powerful experience and at the end I felt as if I had been reborn.'

She stirs the pot of spaghetti sauce as I add the already fried onions and garlic.

'I also love the macrocarpa trees; they are like a painting done by a mad artist. You cannot believe they can be leaning over so much, blown horizontally by the wind. And the Milky Way is so intense and bright it almost makes the other stars disappear. Once when I was going for a walk in the middle of the night, I looked up and couldn't believe it. I had never seen anything like it in Holland. For the first time, I understood the difference between seeing nature and experiencing it.'

'Don't you get lonely?' I query nonchalantly, tossing a salad. 'I mean, four months travelling on your own?' It is a question I am often asked and I am curious as to how she responds.

'Occasionally. It feels good sometimes, to feel sad and lonely.' She slices mushrooms.

'Why would it feel good to feel sadness?'

She stops chopping and stares out of the kitchen window, thinking. 'Because you feel, really feel. It's profound. It reminds you that you can feel emotions; that something can make you feel unhappy. Sometimes you need that sadness and loneliness, after weeks, even months of happiness.'

We watch through the kitchen window as a car pulls up to the end of the driveway. The driver gets out, helps himself to a basket of apples or peaches displayed in an open shed, puts money in a box, and drives off.

She continues: 'It is difficult to remain unchanged tramping around forests and mountains for four months. Walking is a meditative process, it clears the clutter of the mind. Carrying a heavy pack and tramping is a good way to focus your energy on other things, besides the daily worries of life.'

I am consistently amazed at how Europeans such as Lisa can express themselves so well in a second language. The Dutch seem to have a particular ability. 'And you've been happy here?' I ask.

'Happier than ever before. When I left Holland on my own, I was sitting in the airport lounge thinking what a loser I am, travelling with no friends. Now, because I travelled alone, I have more intensely experienced a foreign culture and language in a country far, far away, and discovered an independence and courage I never knew I had before. Now I know better what I want and who I am. I will be happy to continue my studies. Before, it was just an academic exercise.'

Although hitchhiking is free and the backpackers' facilities are competitive and relatively cheap, New Zealand is still a surprisingly expensive country. I wonder how a student could afford to travel here for four months. 'And the money for this trip?' I ask.

'Before, I would be embarrassed to tell anyone what I did to earn enough money to come here. Not now.' She places cutlery on the dining table and returns to find some plates. 'I wanted to come to New Zealand, since I was young; it was a dream. So I took a year off school and for six months' – she hesitates – 'I sorted garbage: plastic, glass, tin. It was a horrible, shit job and smelt very bad, but it paid well. Working there was an insight. The employees in the factory, they did that all their lives, sorting through garbage. I didn't tell them what I was saving money for. I am sure they would understand why, but they just couldn't do it, because they were paying off a mortgage, or a car, or have a family to feed and clothe. That was their life, looking through other people's garbage. It was humbling for me.'

She strains the pasta. We sit down to eat and continue talking. To give particular emphasis to some esoteric philosophical point, I jab my forefinger at the table. The container of margarine is in the line of fire and my finger plunges into it. Unable to believe I have actually done this, I silently remove my greasy digit, hold it in midair and stare at it. Lisa starts giggling, at first subdued, then a bellyaching laugh. It takes the two of us some time to recover our composure.

We settle down to eating again and wipe the tears from our faces. Apropos of nothing, Lisa volunteers in a completely different tone: 'I got a letter from my father today.'

She had been reading a letter earlier, I recall, when I painfully climbed the veranda steps. She holds up the one sheet of paper for me to inspect and then folds it and puts it in its envelope. 'It was a shock.' She places her cutlery on the plate and is suddenly very quiet. Feeling awkward eating on my own, I put my own cutlery down too and wait. 'I've never had a letter from my father before,' she continues. 'I don't feel close to him. Not at all,' she adds, with force. 'I sat down and opened the letter at the post office. I was so nervous about what it would say.' She drops her hands under the table. Her body language has changed, as if she has just crumpled.

She is silent for so long that I have to encourage her to speak again. 'What did your father say?'

She shakes her head and stares out the window, avoiding looking at me. Finally she says, whispering: 'There were only three lines in the letter. He told me how much he envied me, how much he admired my courage in coming here on my own, and how much he loved me and missed me.' Her eyes brim with tears. She plasters a paper towel to her face, covering her eyes.

And then she tells me. I feel the visceral reaction, the nauseous response, as if someone had punched me in the stomach. One reads about sexual abuse in the newspaper. One knows the statistics. I have never heard it from a personal perspective and certainly not in such graphic detail.

I hand her my paper napkin and she uses it to wipe away her tears. We sit opposite each other silently, not eating. Her eyes are downcast. She turns to look over her shoulder at the green orchard outside, her eyes bloodshot, her lower lip gripped between her teeth. She looks so vulnerable, more like a young teenager than an adult.

I feel like putting my arm around her but after what she has just told me, I daren't. We sit there, not saying anything.

When she has recovered, Lisa asks me: 'Where are you going tomorrow?'

'To the kauri forests, then on to the Ninety Mile Beach leading up to Cape Reinga.'

'I am too. Could we do it together?'

I have been looking forward to these last few days in New Zealand and would prefer to be on my own, rather than sharing the end of my trip. But Lisa seems an ideal companion. Not only has she spent the same amount of time in New Zealand as I have, but she has tramped many of the same tracks and more difficult ones as well. We are both feeling nostalgic about our respective departures.

'I like walking on my own during the day,' I reply.

'So do I. We can meet up in the evenings.'

NORTHLAND

I cannot find my sandals anywhere. Lisa, Claes and his two daughters form a search party and hunt for them everywhere, but my sandals are nowhere to be found. It is mysterious. I even phone the last place I stayed, without luck. Finally I tell Claes: 'Don't worry about it. I'm sure they'll turn up somewhere. I'll give you some money to send them on to me, in case you find them.'

We are almost ready to leave when Lisa hands over a plastic bag, whispering: 'Your sandals.'

I open the noticeably cold plastic bag and recoil from the cheesy stench. 'Where did you find them?' I ask, recognising the odour without having to inspect the package closely.

'In the fridge,' she says, deadpan. 'With your food.'

I had wrapped the sandals in an empty plastic grocery bag, because they smelled so bad. I must have absent-mindedly stuffed them in the fridge with my fresh food, which was wrapped in identical plastic bags.

'Do they know?' I nod my head in the direction of the others, who I assume are still searching under beds and sofas.

'That I found your sandals in their fridge?' she asks.

'Yeah,' I reply, looking around to see if they can hear us.

'No, they don't.'

I put a finger to my lips. 'Good. Don't tell them.'

Together we hitchhike from the farm. It feels good setting out together with Lisa. Within minutes of sticking out our thumbs, the first car stops, with an Indian Fijian happily offering a lift. He speaks with an accent distinctive of the Indian sub-continent and tells us without much prompting: 'I emigrated here after the elections in Fiji. The Indian-race party won and the government, with the help of the Fijian-dominated army, took over.' When he smiles, his teeth show brightly against his dark skin. 'I have more Maori friends than pakeha, because they look on me as being "black", like them. I like it here. I bought a house in Auckland, fixed it and sold it at a big profit. With the capital, I have bought an even larger house in Northland.'

He has to check on a blocked drainage ditch on a rural side road, so he lets us off where the road diverts to Dargaville. Lisa and I remove our packs and dump them one behind the other to diminish their profile, so that their bulk doesn't intimidate drivers from picking us up. We stare down the empty road, not so much waiting for a ride as waiting for traffic. We amuse each other by talking, while ever watchful for a car, truck, anything, to come past.

'You hitchhiked all over New Zealand?' I ask.

'Everywhere.'

'On your own?'

'You are the first person I've hitchhiked with,' she replies. 'I've had no problems at all. Would never hitch in Europe though. Too dangerous.'

A Maori stops in a ute. He has someone with him in the cab up front, so he uncovers the back. We climb into the open rear, removing our foam mattresses from our packs to lean against. As he speeds down the winding road, we are painfully thrown against the hard metal, despite the foam mattresses. I grab onto the side with one hand and throw my other arm over Lisa's shoulder, not so much to protect her as to keep us from being thrown into each other or over the side.

The air rushes by. Strands of Lisa's hair are blown loose from the ponytail and flick over her face. She smiles and says: 'I'm really happy.'

'I feel the same.' It makes a big difference having a companion.

199

Despite our frenetic speed, I notice the British publican on the shoulder of the road, plodding relentlessly towards Cape Reinga. I yell into Lisa's ear to explain who he is, as he stares resolutely at the ground in front of him and disappears out of sight.

≶

The Waipoua forest is more like the tropical rainforest of the south-west Pacific than the temperate forests of the rest of New Zealand, with more than three hundred species of trees, shrubs and ferns growing in its protected area. I had been worried that this last walk into the forest might be a disappointment but I need not have been concerned. Just peering into the thick, unspoiled vegetation, I recognise the distinctive sense of tranquillity inspired by the forest's bouquet of scents. I breathe through my nose, mainlining the fragrances of health-restoring trees and plants.

We silently follow a winding duckboard path, as if we were walking on sacred ground. Lisa moves ahead along the raised wooden trail, which curves through forest thick with trees and ferns. The path ends at Tane mahuta, the largest kauri tree left standing in New Zealand. The tree appears to have been there since time immemorial and has the same shape as a gigantic broccoli. High in the branches above is a whole ecological system with scores of different plant species growing out of the thick branches. The trunk is so monolithic that it resembles a stone wall; although its total height is a relatively short fifty-two metres, its girth is thirteen metres and the total volume of the tree a colossal 244 cubic metres. Or so the sign tells us.

You do not need the formality of measurements to understand the might of this living thing. The tree has a powerful presence: it is not hard to imagine why the Maori, in their cosmology, believe that Tane the tree, son of Rangi the sky-father and Papa the earth-mother, physically tore his parents apart, breaking their primal embrace to bring light, space and air into the world. Tane is the life-giver and all living creatures are his children. Even the surrounding bush is in obeisance, granted an audience from an indulgent monarch. Not only is there a sense of power emanating from this majestic tree, but a sense of benevolence as well. As if in a cathedral, we remain silent, paying tribute, touched by the sight of one of God's creations dwarfing us to insignificance. It is a humbling experience.

Lisa whispers into my ear, with the enthusiasm of the academic: 'For the Maori, walking in the forest was sacred, because they believed they were walking among friends and relatives; they think we are all descended from a common source. Unlike the immigrant farmers interested in clearing the land, the Maori were hunters and needed the forest.' She stares fixedly at the massive tree's mottled surface. 'It's hard to believe that the North Island was once covered in these kauri trees. Kauri wood was ideal for building boats, so the European settlers cut down the kauri forests until, a hundred years later, less than half of a per cent of those forests are left standing.'

As we continue our walk, we are confronted by a sign: 'You are in the heart of a small remnant of one of the Earth's most ancient ecosystems. Breathe deeply and tread softly.'

We follow the Yakas Kauri track, pioneered by a Mr Yakas, apparently a gum tapper of some repute. Late-afternoon sun, that strong, bright southern-hemisphere summer light, penetrates the forest canopy, illuminating the dense bush in infinite shades of green. Occasionally, I catch sight of Lisa in front of me as she strides through the thick vegetation. Wading further into the forest, we find ourselves in a grove comprised of scores of kauri trees, six hundred to a thousand years old. Great untapered trunks, like columns, draw the eye up to enormous spreading patterns of leaves in the top canopy. This is what a kauri forest must have looked like before European settlement.

After the grove the path becomes narrow and muddy, winding like a snake through kauri, manuka, rimu trees, kauri grass, ferns and moss. We tramp through this thick, pleasant forest setting, the intense light growing weaker as evening approaches. The friendly atmosphere of the bush becomes sinister as the day evaporates and the distinct shadows in the forest melt into a uniform darkness. It is with a sense of relief that we step out of the dense rainforest into a clearing beside a brook. We immediately set up the tent before swimming in the deep, opaque swimming hole. A cacophony of calls from hidden birds waft from the bush as the last rays of the evening sun cut obliquely down the length of the valley.

Unpacking, we work efficiently as a de facto team, and within minutes, we have a meal cooking; it's a bit like setting up house together. By the time we have finished, the mosquitoes are out in force, huge vampire-like monsters that terrorise us with their bites. Soon after dusk, the air becomes so thick with them that we are driven to seek refuge without cleaning up in the tiny tent. A little voice in my head warns, 'Bad move Andrew,' but I ignore it. Despite the danger of encouraging the marauding possums, we leave out anything that does not need to be protected from rain, such as the dirty pots and pans. Lisa quickly opens the zipper of the tent and we push the packs inside.

'You go first,' she says. 'Hurry, before the mosquitoes get in.'

I dive in to escape the miniature flying hypodermic needles, arrange the hefty packs along one wall of the tent, then lay out the foam mattresses and sleeping-bags.

'You ready yet?' Lisa asks, desperately.

'Yeah,' I reply, shifting around in the cramped space to give her room.

Lisa sticks her head in, but as I turn on my back, her oncoming face connects with my upraised knee. There is an audible crack and her body slumps to the floor of the tent. The mosquitoes take advantage of the opening to invade but she does not move. Considering her desperation a second earlier, this is definitely not a positive sign.

'Are you OK?' I ask idiotically. It is quite evident she is not OK, lying there immobile and probably unconscious.

She stirs, pulling her hands to her face. 'I've broken my glasses.' She rolls over.

'I'm sorry, it was my fault,' I say, hunched over her like a bush version of Quasimodo, the Hunchback of Notre Dame.

'No, it wasn't.' She is more concerned about the mosquitoes swarming in. 'Can you close the zipper?' Her hands hold the remains of her spectacles in place over her face. I crawl over her, close the zipper, and get out my flashlight.

'You're bleeding,' I tell her. One lens of the glasses is broken and there is a gash under her eye where the glass has cut her. Already the cheek is starting to swell. I rummage around until I locate a water bottle and some toilet paper. Here we are, jammed into a one-man tent, crowded out by two large backpacks, with zillions of mosquitoes waiting for us on the other side of the netting and a couple hundred more on the inside happily gorging on our plasma.

'We have to find the pieces of glass first, otherwise we'll cut ourselves.' She puts the broken spectacles back on, holding one hand over her wound. We grope around like a couple of mud wrestlers, as she leads the cramped search, on the floor of the tent and among the folds of our sleeping-bags. Eventually we find all the fragments of glass and I put them in a pocket.

'I'm really sorry,' I tell her.

'It's not your fault.' She lies down on her back. I unwind copious amounts of toilet paper, shakily pour the contents of a water bottle onto it and dab the wet paper on the cut to wipe away the blood. I have to admire her stoicism and I feel guilty, wondering if she needs stitches. How will I get her to a doctor? I am not even sure where we are, nor how far we are from a road. She lies still as I wipe her face, replacing the paper several times until the flow of blood has diminished. It is unbearably hot and close in the tiny tent.

'The bleeding will stop, it's just the fleshy part of my face,' she says, as if allaying my concerns rather than her own.

Eventually, we settle in for the night and lie on top of our sleeping-bags. Occasionally I give her a fresh wad of wet toilet paper, which she keeps plastered to her cheek. We watch the moon rise over the clearing through the mosquito netting. Over the buzzing sound of mosquitoes, I hear strange sounds, almost like the mewing of a kitten. 'Kiwi,' Lisa informs me drowsily, before lapsing into sleep.

During the night, hunting dogs bark in the forest across the river. The howls are menacing, the animals aggressive and excited; in hunting mode, on the trail of a quarry. I feel sorry for the poor, scared creature that has them at its heels. The frenzy of barks reaches a horrible crescendo and there is the grim crack of a rifle shot echoing across the valley, then silence.

I listen to the unfamiliar sounds, unable to nod off. My mind is too agitated, my imagination running wild with each unidentified noise outside the tent. Even if there aren't any killer wild animals out there, there are plenty of people with guns and bloodthirsty dogs.

Later, a noise wakes me, and I see a devilish face peering down at me through the mosquito netting. I scream.

It is only a possum, not the Kiwi equivalent of an inbred Appalachian lunatic, and the poor harmless marsupial squeals a fiendish alarm back at me. My own hollering wakes Lisa up and she screams too, encouraging the frightened possum to emit more diabolical screeches before it ambles away.

'Must have been a possum,' I explain in the ensuing silence.

'Just a possum?' she asks, incredulous. 'It sounded horrible.' She does not realise I contributed my own terrified screams to the possum's effort.

'I think it has gone now,' I add, recovering from my own fright.

Exhausted, we sleep well past dawn. In the morning light Lisa looks as if she has been badly beaten up, the cut not as visible as the swelling just below the eye. We pack up the tent and sleeping-bags and walk out of the forest to the road, where we stand patiently, thumbs out. Two young boys cycle up to us and stop, sitting astride their bikes, unabashedly staring at Lisa's battered face.

'What happened?' one of them asks her.

She looks over at me, just the trace of a smile on her face. 'Ask him what happened.'

'Got attacked by a possum in the middle of the night.'

'Possums don't do that,' the more vocal of the two boys exclaims.

'Well, she walked into the door of the tent. How about that?'

He screws up his face, unsure what to make of the absurd explanation.

A car pulling a trailer with a motorbike stops to pick us up, thankfully cutting short any further questions from the two boys. We load our gear and some hours later are dropped off beside a lagoon, where the ebbing tide has left an expanse of mudflats and mangrove trees. Spying a treasure trove of gigantic oysters, Lisa and I slide through the slippery, oily mud to where the oysters cling to young mangrove stems. I pry one of them open with my Swiss army knife and pass it to Lisa. We shuck and lustily slurp down dozens of oysters, each the size and consistency of an uncooked egg yolk.

With our hands bleeding from the sharp edges of the shells, we plop out of the mud and return to the road. Our sandals and legs are caked with mud, as if we are wearing gumboots. The mud cracks, drying in the tropical heat of the day as we walk towards a backpackers lodge hidden in the trees.

Phil the owner is originally from Australia. He shows us around his lodge, which is built like a tree house. It looks like something out of *Winnie-the-Pooh*.

I ask him: 'How do you like living in New Zealand?'

He waxes lyrical: 'It's so unspoilt here and the Maori are a wonderful people. There are so many things us pakeha could learn from the Maori.'

'For example?' I ask, as he shows off his library full of books on New Zealand.

'Well, the *tangihanga*, their show of respect for the dead. It's very moving. The funeral ceremony is three days long. The body lies in the *marae* building in an open coffin. Visitors *hongi* the deceased as a sign there is life after death, then greetings are shared and a feast of roasted pig or beef or sheep commences to celebrate *whakanoa*, the freeing of the spirit. They take it in turns to hold a sacred stick and make a speech. Everyone ends up sleeping in the *marae*. The family doesn't have to pay for anything: all the costs are borne by friends who come from miles around to attend the funeral and pay their respects. At the end of the three days, people have had time to accept the death. By the third day, many of the speeches have a humorous tone to them.' He pauses. 'Trouble is, they don't give each other the same respect when they are alive. The physical and mental abuse of wives and children is terrible. I worked as a volunteer ambulance attendant for ten years before giving up in frustration. You would not believe the violence around here. And their other big problem: the infighting among themselves. You've heard of the tall poppy syndrome? That describes the Maori when one of them gets successful.'

Lisa elects to sleep in her tent in a pasture, avoiding my bony knees or any potential aphrodisiacal effects from the oysters, though she says it is to save money. I choose a more comfortable bed and Phil leads me to a spotless room with a view of the harbour.

He continues talking, while pointing out the landmarks. 'There was a young Maori guy here. He started up a business taking tourists in kayaks around the harbour, the mangrove trees, old Maori sites.' Phil indicates each area. 'He did everything right. He checked with the Maori elders, got approval from DOC. He did his research, knew his stuff, and started taking European tourists out on kayaking excursions. The tourists loved it and he was successful. Then the green-eyed monster of jealousy raised its ugly head. The local *marae* told him they wanted a cut of his profits. He refused. They told him he wasn't from their area, he was a Maori from East Cape, a different tribe and they wanted him to stop. He replied that at least he was a Maori. They stopped him operating anyway.

'A year later, some highly paid consultants, whose salaries were funded by the government, came here from Auckland to study the area and advise the unemployed Maori on potential business opportunities. They did their research, then met with the community, to discuss with them how the area was an ideal place to give ecotours; for example kayaking trips to old Maori sites. There was an uncomfortable silence in the hall. The East Cape Maori was there in the audience.' Phil shakes his head at the memory of it all. 'How do you deal with that kind of jealousy?' he asks rhetorically.

He indicates a different area with a sweep of his hand. 'Now a white man operates more or less the same tour, very successfully, but he doesn't go into the Maori areas and he doesn't pay them anything. That's what I mean. One Maori pulls himself out of the morass of 80 per cent unemployment and the others are sitting on the sidelines just waiting to drag him down to their level again. It's pathetic, but that's the way it is. If the Maori could get themselves organised, they could start a *pa*, give cultural tours to the travellers passing through the area, especially for the Europeans, who seem to be the most interested. But they can't seem to break out of this world of apathy, and so they sit there collecting the dole, losing their self-respect, drinking and abusing one another.'

I follow as he shows me around the property. 'Don't get me wrong. I love the Maori, I've a lot of time for them. It's just such a shame to see so many opportunities lost because they squabble among themselves. It's so frustrating to witness. We don't create a product to cater to visitors interested in the history and culture of New Zealand, and so we encourage the kind of tourist who doesn't care.' We climb down the stairs out of the tree house to the main building.

'Sometimes I see young visitors on the backpacker buses. They cross the harbour on the ferry where you have a beautiful view of the hills, the church and historic buildings. It's easy to imagine what it was like one hundred years ago when there would be thirty schooners anchored, waiting to load up with kauri gum or logs or timber. But nowadays, you'll see all these young passengers intently playing cards on the bus, or sleeping off their hangovers, not even vaguely interested in what's going on around them. At the end of the day, if we can't cater to the more ecologically and culturally sensitive traveller, we'll end up with tourists coming here for the drinking, bungee jumping and jet boating. But they can do that anywhere, and we'll have lost an opportunity to have a tourist industry that encourages Kiwis to examine their own traditions.'

Tomorrow, Lisa and I will continue up to Cape Reinga, where Te Moana-a-Rehua, the man-sea of the Maori, the colder and rougher Tasman Sea, meets the woman-sea, Te Tai-o-Whitirea, the Pacific Ocean. I sit in Phil's library and read about Northland. To the Maori, Cape Reinga is known as Te Rerenger Wairua, leaping place of the spirits. It was here, the Maori believed, the dead should depart the island to rejoin their ancestors in the half-mythical island known as Hawaiki.

The books in the library whet my appetite to walk up to this last point of land where my trip will end. I feel sentimental about my departure. Although I have been travelling for four months, sleeping in a different bed almost every night, I am not tired, nor fed up. New Zealand is growing on me.

~

It takes us no time to hitch to Kaitaia, our staging point for Ninety Mile Beach. Hurtling along the road, we look vainly for the Brit soldiering his way northwards. Lisa and I shop for food at a local supermarket and loaded with supplies we walk to the backpackers lodge. In the afternoon we draw the curtains in the lounge and watch the video of *Once Were Warriors*.

That evening, Lisa suggests: 'Want to go to one of the local Maori pubs and find out for ourselves what it's like?'

We head off to a Kaitaia pub where the local clientele is mostly Maori. Two men arm-wrestle at a stand-up table. One has a tattoo of a skull on his neck; his opponent has 'Maori' tattooed on his forehead. They look formidable with their pumped-up Popeye muscled arms. They all greet us warmly enough though, and smile amiably.

The violent images from the film we have just seen hardly seem applicable to these friendly people. A group of Maori women join the table of arm-wrestlers. While the men have become bloated through years of beer consumption, many of the women are quite skeletal, with haggard looks which make them look old beyond their years. One has a badly broken nose. Guiltily, I realise Lisa fits in here, with her swollen black eye and cut face. She smiles at the people around her, and a man comes over to chat her up.

A sofa-sized man in his late fifties enters the bar and sidles up to me. 'I don't know them,' he says, indicating the rest of the Maori in the bar, most of whom appear the worse for drink. 'But if they tell me they are unemployed, then I have no sympathy for them. If you've got two arms and two legs' – he holds out his worn hands – 'and a head on your shoulders, then don't give me this shit about the world being against you. Everyone has obstacles in front of them. You climb over them' – he gesticulates with his hands – 'or around them, but don't sit back on the dole feeling sorry for yourself . . .' He lets the sentence hang in the air before continuing: 'They say 90 per cent of prisoners in jail are Maori. They also tell us, with respect to land rights, that there are no full-blooded Maoris left in New Zealand today. Well then, I can tell you how to change those statistics with just the stroke of a pen.'

'How?' I ask. I am overshadowed by his ironing-board shoulders on one side of me, and the huge Maori chatting up Lisa on the other.

'The pakeha say there are no full-blooded Maoris. Then why don't they admit that most prisoners are half English, a lot are half Scottish or Irish or Dalmatian, instead of saying the jails are so full of bloody Maoris?'

NINETY MILE BEACH – CAPE MARIA VAN DIEMEN – CAPE REINGA

While standing on the gravel shoulder, waiting for a ride up towards Ninety Mile Beach, we read a DOC pamphlet that Lisa has bought:

The whole of the northern tip of the North Island is steeped in
Maori tradition. It is, in fact, the most spiritually significant area in
the country, for it is here that after death all Maori spirits travel to
the pohutukawa tree on the headland of Cape Reinga and descend
into the underworld (Reinga) by sliding down a root to fall into the
sea below. They climb out again on Ohaua, the highest point of the
Three Kings Islands, to bid their last farewell before returning to
the land of their ancestors.

Three Maori loggers give us a ride in their truck. They are
exhausted, and don't say a word; even the driver seems to be
asleep, his eyes almost closed. They drop us off at a petrol station
where we are picked up by an American woman who tells us the
minute details of her life, non-stop, for the forty-five minutes we
are with her. I barely listen to her autobiography and keep a lookout for the walking British publican. I believe I am going to beat
him to the top, even if it has taken the two of us four months to
get here from the bottom of the South Island.

We are dropped off at Te Paki stream, already more than
halfway up Ninety Mile Beach. Lisa observes: 'Almost the only
words we said during the ride were to thank her at the end. She
has no idea where we are from or who we are. We could write a
short biography on her. We know the names of her children, her
husband, why she took six months off from her family to wander
around New Zealand, what she does for a living and why she
quit.'

'She just needs some time and space, someone to listen to her.
She's sorting it all out. She'll be OK.'

It is drizzling, almost like a heavy mist, which cuts down on
the glare and heat from the sun. On a clear day it must be unbearably hot walking across these mountains of dunes. The sand
underfoot is slightly damp, rendering it more compact and relatively easy to climb. The moisture brings out the colour of the
darker grains of sand, which are patterned like beautifully stained
wood. From the top of a dune we can barely see through the mist
and over the humps of sand to the indistinct grey ocean beyond.
Winding south-east is Te Paki stream, recognisable even from a
distance as a line of green vegetation, which acts as an effective

barrier to the encroachment of the dunes further inland. We leave the interior behind, the green paddocks dotted with heavy trees, contrasting strangely with the barren coastal dunes rising 150 metres high. At the top of a dune I wait for Lisa, who emerges from the drizzle and desolation like a character from a classic movie.

When Lisa had asked me if I wanted to join her on the walk up to Ninety Mile Beach, I had been ambivalent. On reflection, it is appropriate that I share this final walk with another tramper. All these months I have walked alone and met up with other foreign trampers in the evening. It is fitting now that I finish my odyssey the same way.

'So we agree then to stay within sight of one another until we stop for lunch, and to break camp?' I ask. I am worried she might remember her swollen eye and abandon me to the elements, my imagination and the possums. Although she has the tent, I have the cooking gear and most of the food.

'Yes,' she replies. 'I prefer to walk in front. Shall we make a direct line for the ocean?'

'Once we get to Ninety Mile Beach, we head north along the coast. Should be easy enough.' I look around at the scenery. The vague forms of dunes are dreamlike, adding to the ambience and heightening my nostalgia about this trip. After four months of wandering around New Zealand, my journey is ending. 'Let's take our time so we can enjoy it. We can stop whenever and wherever we want. We have everything we need with us.'

She agrees, striding down the slope of the dune and into the mist, leaving me following in her tracks. The desert landscape is featureless except for the ridgelines into which Lisa disappears. With the swirling mist and slight rainfall, there is a sense of transition, of passing into an ethereal world. The sand is devoid of life and the sea gives off what I imagine is an odour of death: a kind of a stale smell. It is easy to imagine how the Maori thought their spirits wandered up this desolate coast before moving on to an afterlife.

I lose sight of Lisa in the folds of dunes and cannot find her footsteps in the damp sand. It is not so much that it is difficult to follow her trail; rather, it is because I have not been concentrating, so lost am I in my own world of thoughts. This sense of isolation is abruptly shattered when I climb over the last small dune overlooking Ninety Mile Beach. Lisa is standing on the beach, staring at me with her mouth open, eyes wide in astonishment. Up and down the flat expanse of beach are hundreds of utes and thousands of fishermen standing deep in the surf, casting with long fishing rods into the ocean waves. She laughs when she sees my look of disbelief. We thought we were experiencing a special sense of wilderness isolation and spirituality, but the reality is that we are in a sandpit surrounded by a thousand happy Kiwi fishermen.

I slide out of the dunes onto Ninety Mile Beach. A fisherman steps from under the canvas tarpaulin stretched from the back of his ute and stares at me. The back gate of the ute is open and a gas stove with several burners sits on top, supplied by a large tank of gas. Fatty food cooks noisily on the stove.

His frying pan contains eggs floating like life rafts in a sea of fat, with bits of charred bacon clinging on like desperate survivors. 'Steak, eggs and bacon. Want some?' he asks, appraising our lean backpacks.

'No thanks. Why are there so many fishermen? There must be thousands of you.'

'Fishing contest for the best snapper,' he replies, flipping the eggs. Despite the overcast weather, his face is florid and burnt to a crispy red. The ute faces the sea, providing shelter against the prevailing wind. He has dug a pit behind the vehicle so he can use the tailgate as a table. It is a mobile bach.

'You camping here?' I ask.

'Nah, we fish different stretches of the beach each day.'

'It looks like a lot of work setting it all up just for the day,' Lisa observes.

'Yeah, but it's cold in the sea, so it's worth it,' he explains. One of the fishermen waddles up from the surf, pulling at the shoulder straps of his wetsuit. He examines us, with our heavy backpacks and hiking boots, as if we were astronauts. He pulls the top of the wetsuit off and puts on a T-shirt with the motto 'Groper all day long' printed on the back.

Eager to move on, we thread our way through the line of vehicles. A sizeable ray and a small shark are either stranded on the sand, or more likely have been thrown there after being caught. We walk to the end of the official fishing area, marked by a Land Rover with a flag advertising beer waving from an antenna.

'This the end of the fishing area?' I ask the long-haired Maori man cutting bait on the bonnet of the vehicle.

'Yeah,' he replies, not bothering to look at us.

'Seems a lot of the fishermen are pretty far out into the surf,' Lisa observes.

He looks up at the waves, which almost engulf some of the anglers casting their lines into the waves. 'Yeah, had to rescue five of them yesterday. Got pulled out by the rip-tide.'

'How'd you rescue them?'

'Rescue teams drive up and down the beach with a boat. As soon as someone gets sucked out, we radio for them and they come and reel him in.'

'Must be dangerous,' Lisa says.

'Yeah.'

'All that for a snapper the size of a big shoe,' she adds, a comment more intended for herself than anyone else.

'Some are a lot bigger than that,' the Maori says.

We continue walking to the end of the beach, to Scott Point, which is marked by a rocky peninsula. The tide is out, revealing a carpet of mussels clinging onto the exposed shoreline, growing so thickly, mussel on mussel, it is impossible to see the bare rock underneath.

'Let's make lunch,' I suggest. 'One of those pasta dishes, with seafood pictured on the packet. We can boil up the mussels and mix them with the pasta.'

We scramble along the rocky promontory to find the biggest, fattest mussels. Within minutes, we have collected more than enough in our two pots. We fill the pots with water and find a cave offering protection from the strong onshore winds. It is some twenty metres deep and ten metres high.

'I hope this isn't one of those caves where the Maori used to leave their dead,' Lisa worries. 'It feels like it.' We look around the natural cavity, but the only things living are crabs and huge spiders suspended in silver webs hanging from the roof. It smells like death; the same smell as earlier.

Lisa says: 'It's eerie in here, let's get out, I don't like the feeling. I think there are ghosts.'

Safely outside the cave, we attach the gas canisters to both of our stoves, boiling water for the pasta and mussels. Placed in the boiling water, the mussels open, revealing succulent apricot-coloured flesh. We extract the meat from the shells and mix it with the pasta, adding the powdered flavouring. Mixed with a kilo of fresh mussels, the pasta actually tastes of seafood for the first time.

We wash the pots, scouring them with sand, repack and ascend the rocky peninsula. It is half-submerged in drifting dunes and we follow a trail through manuka bush. Lisa soon outpaces me. At the top of the rise, I have a view back over the long pale stretch of Ninety Mile Beach, which is almost disguised by the mist, light drizzle and wind-blown spray off the ocean. Despite the grey day, the ocean is turquoise-coloured, dotted near the shore with wet-suited anglers standing as far out in the surf as they dare. I continue north, arbitrarily choosing a footpath, and eventually reach a dead end overlooking a cliff, with the ocean surging below. Not about to cast myself off the cliff like a lemming, I retrace my steps.

In the distance, I recognise Lisa, returning to retrieve me. When she sees me, she stops and waits before turning around to continue her trek. This time I concentrate, making sure I can see her in front of me each time there is a fork in the route.

From the rocks the track descends to Twilight Beach. Far ahead, I see Lisa's solitary figure. Her soggy footprints disappear as the incoming fan of waves wash over the beach. Her reflection is absorbed in the sandy wetness like ink in blotting paper. A breeze blows, mimicking the whispering of Maori spirits urging us onward towards the end of our journey. Black oystercatchers strut on the beach with the authority of diminutive funeral directors. Line upon line of waves cascade endlessly as ocean crests rise and then tumble in a froth of foaming bubbles. The setting and subdued light lend a moody, almost melancholic feel to this beautiful land.

Lisa waits silently for me at the far end of the beach, where we climb a sandy hill into another desert of dunes. As we reach the top, we can see the Cape Maria van Diemen peninsula protruding into the Tasman Sea to the west. To the north-east, at Cape Reinga, the Pacific Ocean meets the Tasman Sea in a maelstrom of turbulence. The waters are wildly chaotic, mountainous spumes rising from the depths, dynamically imitating in liquid form the folds of sand dunes we had crossed getting to Ninety Mile Beach. Supernatural forces seem to mysteriously heave these turgid waters, and it is easy to understand why the Maori imagined that the spirits of the dead departed Aotearoa from Cape Reinga, descending into the ocean through the roots of the spirit tree. I want to point out the surging waves to Lisa, who is already some distance ahead of me. I yell out aloud, 'Lisa, Lisa!' but the wind flings my futile cries back at me.

She waits and together we cross a narrow spit tenuously linking Cape Maria van Diemen to the mainland, then set up the tent in the lee of a grassy hill on the peninsula. The short tent pegs are useless in the loose sand and I scavenge dry sticks to pin the corners of the tent down. The light from the stippled sunset sky is absorbed into the dunes, so that they seem to radiate pastel colours.

We descend to the beach. The tide is high and the waves tilt dangerously; steep liquid walls collapsing in ugly curls. The blue water of the incoming crests turns a messy beige as the waves crash and the rip-tide tugs violently at the sandy shore. I strip and walk into the receding surf only to hear Lisa yell out loud: 'Please don't go swimming!'

Although I am only up to my knees in the water, the water pulls at me fiercely, like fists clasped tightly around my ankles.

The sand vanishes from under my feet as it is swept out with the retreating surge. Another wave threatens to inundate me, and like a kid, I run out of harm's way. It becomes a game, following the receding wave, squatting in the ebbing water to sluice myself, then retreating rapidly back up the beach before the next monstrous wave catches up to me. Lisa joins in, and we play hide-and-seek with the tentacles of the ocean.

Exhausted and getting cold, we climb back up the beach to the tent, on the way finding a wooden crate and a heavy worn plank of driftwood. We haul the scavenged firewood back up with us. While Lisa prepares dinner, I find stones to support the plank, to make a bench seat; then I break apart the small crate, cut wood shavings off the plank and light a fire. It is so windy we must sit huddled together on the bench, which is on the windward side of the fire, to prevent it from blowing out. The warm breeze keeps the mosquitoes and sand flies at bay. Although there is a breeze, the night is not cold; the temperature is perfect.

We fill our empty stomachs with hot pasta mixed with tinned tuna. Satiated, we sit transfixed by the flames and coals, not talking. I neatly fold slats of unburned crate onto itself so that the unburned ends catch alight. The fire crackles. We sit staring thoughtfully at the glowing, pulsating embers. Above, a black sky is permeated with innumerable stars. Neither of us says anything. It is our last night camping out, before heading towards Auckland to catch our respective planes home.

'Are you sad to be leaving New Zealand?' I ask eventually, breaking the comfortable silence.

'Yes. I could think of making my home here, easily,' Lisa replies.

I use a stick to assemble the last bits of burning embers in a heap, to keep them alight, and will them to continue burning.

'And you?' she asks.

I take my time before replying. It isn't easy to neatly encapsulate the thoughts that have distilled whilst walking in the rainforests of New Zealand these months. I focus on one of the small remnants of burning wood as it glows brightly with a waft of the ocean breeze. 'I like this country and its people. I have ties to another world, not a lot, but they would be difficult to sever by moving so far away. It's possible. More than anything, this journey has given me time to reflect, a luxury few Westerners have.' Lisa nods, once, just enough to encourage me to keep talking. 'We are so busy making money to make our lives comfortable that we do not have time to just *be*.'

A piece of wood flares briefly before it turns into a chunk of black carbon. I study the core of the charcoal where the last purple flames still flicker. We do not move for a long time, still sitting huddled together protecting our hearth from the breeze, until the last vestige of orange warmth has gone from the fire. When the flames and burning embers finally subside, there is an overwhelming sense of isolation. The black ocean is almost 360 degrees around us; we are tenuously connected to the North Island by a narrow strip of sand. It seems we are far, far removed from the rest of the world.

Reluctantly, we bury the leftover blackened wood in the sand, then manoeuvre into the tiny tent. We lie on top of our sleeping-bags, heads by the entrance, staring out at the dunes and the moonless, inky-black sky salted with stars. I recognise the Southern Cross and Orion's belt. Even with only the stars for illumination, there is sufficient silvery light to cast shadows. The tent flap is open; there is no need to zipper the mosquito netting closed.

This is our last night on the tracks of New Zealand. Tomorrow we will walk up to Cape Reinga.

During the night, I wake up. The two of us are sleeping on our sides, facing each other. There is so little space in the tent that our foreheads are touching and Lisa's hand rests on my arm. It feels good. I fall back asleep again without stirring.

The hissing of the pressurised gas canister wakes me. Lisa is up already, boiling water for tea. I have slept so soundly I did not notice her crawl out of the tent. The sun is not yet over the horizon and the pre-dawn colours are muted.

We break camp. 'Are you OK?' I ask her, as we load up.

'I'm just sad,' she replies.

I look around to make sure we have left nothing behind. 'About leaving this place?'

'About everything,' she says, looking out at the turbulence where the two oceans meet. She talks quietly, almost as if she were in a trance. 'During the night, I woke up. We were lying so close to each other. It didn't feel bad.'

I cannot see her eyes, cannot read what she is saying between the lines. I look up the deserted beach, feel the breeze blowing in from the ocean.

Walking side by side, we cross the narrow spit of sand from Cape Maria van Diemen, along a path which leads up over a dune separating this beach from the last open stretch before the cape. We are following the same route the Maori spirits take on their way up to Cape Reinga. From the top of the sand hill we can see a long line of curving dunes in the foreground, and then a bright green, flourishing paddock beyond, with dark forested hills behind. It is a strange landscape, this juxtaposition of life and death, the verdant and the barren.

We descend to another beach, the last stretch of sandy coastline before rocky Cape Reinga. The day is bright in contrast to the moodiness of yesterday. The frothing crest of waves catches the sunlight gaily.

'Lisa?'

'Yes.'

'Shall we continue together back down to Auckland?'

She puts her hand on my shoulder as we walk.

The morning sun comes out from behind a puffball cloud, its light catching another line of waves cascading on the beach. The surf is long and gentle, rhythmically curling and collapsing. The day is bursting full with colour. As we approach the end of the beach, we see an odd-looking character in gumboots walking up and down the edge of the waves, occasionally bending to pick something up. He is so intent that he does not notice us. When we get closer, I can see that he carries a traditional carved Maori walking stick and a leather hat with a wide brim. On his back is what looks like a homemade knapsack made out of flax.

'What are you looking for?' I ask in greeting, startling him.

'Offerings,' the Maori replies. His long black hair is pulled back in a ponytail.

'Offerings?' Lisa queries.

'Yeah. Gifts.' He smiles.

'What kind of gifts?' she asks, curious.

'Ah yeah, paua shells, feathers, cat's-eyes, that kind of thing.'

He holds out a worn calcified button. Lisa examines the tiny white object. 'What's that?'

'It's a cat's-eye. From a shell. It's like a lid; when the flesh goes in the shell this hatch protects it. See?' he holds it up for us to inspect, pointing out the spiralling lines with a worn and dirty thumbnail. 'It's the seed of life. In the middle it starts from nothing and goes in circles until it comes out here. Just like life. Worth heaps if you can find them, eh.'

'To whom?' Lisa questions.

'To the spirits,' he replies, putting it back in his pocket.

'The spirits?'

'Yeah, the spirits. The spirits of our dead ancestors.' He glances out at the ocean where the mountains of waves jostle dramatically.

'What are you going to do with your gifts?'

'Take them up to the spirit tree.' He points with his eyes at the Cape. 'Put the offering in its roots.'

'The one at the end of Cape Reinga?'

'That's the one.'

'Why?' Lisa enquires.

'Spirit tree's sick.' The smile disappears.

'How do you know?' I ask.

'Heaps of spirits can't escape,' he replies, pulling more cat's-eyes from his bulging pockets. Lisa leans forward to study the handful.

'Where are they?'

'Stuck in caves along the coast.'

She looks at me and I know she is thinking about the lunch we nearly had in the spooky cave. 'They escape through the roots of the spirit tree?' Lisa cross-examines.

'Yeah.' He nods his head.

'And they can't now because it's sick?' she asks, looking at him.

'Yeah.'

'Makes sense to me.'

I agree, thinking back over these last months. The rainforests and this desolate coastline had seemed spiritual places full of the ghosts of the Maori and other denizens of the underworld. I didn't realise they were trying to escape; I thought they lived there.

'My name is Wayne, Wayne Running Boots.' He holds out a hand; his grip is tight and firm. He smiles broadly. Several of his teeth are missing.

'Running Boots sounds like a North American Indian name,' I observe.

'Yeah, I got heaps of North American Indian friends. Met them at a conference of aboriginal peoples. Where you from?' he asks me.

'Canada.'

'Ah yeah.'

'Where are you from?' I ask, curious.

He laughs, takes off the tatty hat and scratches his scalp, then shrugs, replacing the hat. 'Nowhere. Just sleep out. Wherever I sleep, that's home.' Sounds familiar. 'Just walked from Bluff to Cape Reinga now. Done it three, four times. Walked everywhere.' Another one.

'That's why they call you Running Boots?'

'Yeah.' He laughs self-consciously and lifts one of his gum-boots to show us the sole. The original patterned tread has worn away.

'Did you meet an Englishman walking up from Invercargill? He's walking the length of New Zealand too.'

Running Boots shakes his head. 'Ain't seen no one else.'

'You just sleep out all the time?' Lisa asks.

'Yeah. Came up Spirits Bay on the other side, then slept out at Tapotupotu beach.'

He takes his leave, climbing the steep path leading from the beach to the top of the rock promontory of Cape Reinga. Lisa and I dump our packs in the shade of the overhanging rocks at the edge of the beach. The tide is ebbing. We strip and wade into the sea, occasionally looking for Wayne Running Boots as he climbs the hillside.

There is no rip-tide here and the shelf of beach reaches far into the long line of waves coming in from the sea. We dare go further out and body-surf, catching the rollers that return us to shallow water. We swim out repeatedly, ducking under the incoming waves. Each time we dive, it is as if we are being ritually cleansed. Waves topple over us as we submerge under them, to swim back out to deeper water and body-surf in again. The sun is brilliant and warm, the sea a bright turquoise. A dozen dolphins ride the swells briefly before disappearing. Their presence is a reminder of all that is wonderful about New Zealand.

We leave the beach and follow in the footsteps of Wayne Running Boots. At the top of the peninsula are several concrete block buildings. One is a tiny shop selling souvenirs, postcards, ice creams and soft drinks. Several coaches are parked in the parking lot, and more turn up as we watch. Tourists congregate at the bottleneck of the only door to the shop, most with name tags on their chests. I am tempted to greet them all by name. 'Hey Joe!' or '*Sayonara* Hashimoto!' Many seem to have picnic boxes; they munch through their contents while sitting on benches. Others wander around taking photographs, or buying souvenirs. A Japanese man strolls about quietly, commenting aloud to his video camera, recording both his voice and the view of his wife as he carefully studies a built-in miniature screen. They look so clean and colourful. Lisa and I seem out of place as we stroll among them with our dirty clothing, heavy backpacks and hiking boots.

We follow the crowd of tourists the short distance along a smooth asphalt path to a small lighthouse. A signpost points in different directions with the distance to cities marked: Tokyo, Los Angeles, Sydney, Vancouver and London. Three tourists stand by the signpost happily mugging it up for the photographer.

I look around for the English publican, almost expecting to see him sitting there quietly on his own, contemplating whatever it is that instigated his walk up the length of New Zealand. He is nowhere to be seen.

Far out to sea, a cruise ship slowly passes by the northern tip of New Zealand, its sleek hull silhouetted dark against the sun reflecting off the shimmering ocean. Closer in, the waves of the Pacific Ocean and the Tasman Sea clash and dance dramatically. Immediately below is Cape Reinga, but the tourists do not seem to notice. While the lighthouse has an information plaque on it, there is no marker describing this most sacred of Maori sites.

Staring down at the craggy crevices, I make out the pohutukawa tree clinging miraculously to the bare rocks. Waves surge and foam about its roots. It does not seem possible that an unprotected tree could survive amidst these exposed rocks, which are relentlessly hammered by the sea. Yet it has survived, not for a day, but for hundreds of years. Then I notice amongst the twisted tangle of rocks and roots the figure of Wayne Running Boots. He is bent on his knees, humbly proffering shells and feathers and cat's-eyes to the spirit tree.

NEW ZEALAND

This practical guide introduces the spectacular natural wonders, rich Maori culture and friendly people of New Zealand. If you're after adventure, get ready for an adrenalin rush – from climbing mighty Mount Cook to kayaking along an underground river or rap jumping from an Auckland skyscraper.

- 113 detailed maps, including national parks and ski areas
- extensive background information on Maori history and culture
- accommodation options from scenic camping grounds to down-to-earth farmstays to classy B&Bs
- exhaustive coverage of outdoor activities
- colour flora and fauna section
- Maori and New Zealand English language sections

TRAMPING IN NEW ZEALAND

With detailed descriptions ranging from family walks to hard high-level routes, advice on when to go and how to do it, detailed and reliable maps and background information, this informative guide is an invaluable resource for both independent walkers and those in an organised group – in fact, for anyone who believes that the best way to see the world is on foot.

LONELY PLANET JOURNEYS

JOURNEYS is a unique collection of travel writing – published by the company that understands travel better than anyone else.

It is a series for anyone who has ever experienced – or dreamed of – the magical moment when they encountered a strange culture or saw a place for the first time. They are tales to read while you're planning a trip, while you're on the road or while you're in an armchair, in front of a fire.

These outstanding titles explore our planet through the eyes of a diverse group of international writers. JOURNEYS books catch the spirit of a place, illuminate a culture, recount an adventure, or introduce a fascinating way of life. They always entertain, and always enrich the experience of travel.

'Lively, intelligent and varied . . . an important contribution to travel literature' – *Age (Melbourne)*

LONELY PLANET UNPACKED
Travel Disaster Stories
By Tony Wheeler and other Lonely Planet Writers

Every traveller has a horror story to tell: lost luggage, bad weather, illness or worse. In this lively collection of travel disaster tales, Lonely Planet writers share their worst moments of life on the road.

From Kenya to Sri Lanka, from Brazil to Finland, from the Australian outback to India, these travellers encounter hurricanes, road accidents, secret police and nasty parasites. Reading these funny and frightening stories from the dark side of the road will make you think twice about a career as a travel writer, but the best thing about them is the knowledge that it all happened to somebody else . . .